THE
REICHSTAG
FIRE

THE
REICHSTAG
FIRE
THE CASE AGAINST THE
NAZI CONSPIRACY

SVEN FELIX KELLERHOFF

TRANSLATED BY KARINA BERGER

The
History
Press

Originally published in German as *Der Reichstagsbrand*, 2008
This English language edition first published 2016

The History Press
The Mill, Brimscombe Port
Stroud, Gloucestershire, GL5 2QG
www.thehistorypress.co.uk

© be. bra verlag, Berlin-Brandenburg, 2008

English translation © Karina Berger, 2016

The right of Sven Felix Kellerhoff, to be identified as the Author
of this work has been asserted in accordance with the
Copyright, Designs and Patents Act 1988.

British Library Cataloguing in Publication Data.
A catalogue record for this book is available from the British Library.

ISBN 978 0 7509 6487 6

Typesetting and origination by The History Press
Printed and bound by CPI Group (UK) Ltd

CONTENTS

PREFACE TO THE ENGLISH EDITION

The ritual is always the same: at the beginning of each year, by mid-February at the latest, a string of articles, sometimes even entire books, are published about the Reichstag fire that took place on the evening of 27 February 1933. Nearly all of these publications, almost invariably written by the same group of authors, claim to contain 'new insights' or 'new interpretations' about the arson attack that had the most serious consequences in world history. For this is exactly what the flames in the German parliament building, exactly four weeks after Hitler's appointment as Reich chancellor, turned out to be: a fiery signal for the Nazi dictatorship that proved so disastrous for Germany and Europe, and cost millions of people their lives.

Almost all of these articles and books have something else in common: they present supposed inconsistencies, alleged suspects or so-called facts which have in fact been known for decades. The latest book by the American historian Benjamin Carter Hett, published in 2014, is a case in point.

Burning the Reichstag: An Investigation into the Third Reich's Enduring Mystery is nothing but an indictment, containing not a single new argument or piece of evidence. Those who are familiar with the extensive body of literature on the topic will be very surprised to see that Hett revisits several well-known claims that have long been refuted. In his desire to prove the National Socialists' role in the arson attack, he cites practically every piece of 'evidence', no matter how absurd.

Now, working with a hypothesis is certainly a valid approach. Of course one can support the assumption that the National Socialists set the Reichstag on fire as an excuse to brutally enforce their dictatorship. However, historical scholarship is ultimately based on sources: hypotheses that consistently contradict undoubtedly genuine sources are of no use and are excluded from serious discourse. Usually, this works rather well – except in the case of the Reichstag fire.

For instance, in his book, Hett names Hans Georg 'Heini' Gewehr as the possible perpetrator around 200 times. Now, it is true that Hans-Bernd Gisevius, a former Gestapo officer and later self-proclaimed resistance fighter against Hitler, claimed that Gewehr was responsible for the crime during the Nuremberg Trials for major war criminals in 1945. However, Gisevius, one of the great storytellers about the Third Reich, was forced to retract his main allegations, as there was no evidence whatsoever. The claim that Hans Georg Gewehr was part of a Nazi stormtrooper [the *Sturmabteilung*, or SA] arsonist commando is quite simply made up.

Yet this does not seem to be a problem for Benjamin Hett, or any of the other authors who, again and again, write about the events and the consequences of 27 February 1933, who rehash the well-known conspiracy theories that have already been debunked several times. This book, however, takes a different approach. Based on fifteen years of research, and a thorough and unbiased analysis of the case file, it investigates the criminal case of the Reichstag fire; in other words, its 'career'.

This book explains what really happened on that cold Monday evening in Berlin. It uncovers how the belief that the Nazis were the culprits established itself – a belief that runs contrary to all available facts, but that is encouraged by all the other terrible crimes they committed. This book also takes Marinus van der Lubbe's repeated confession seriously. It is not the first book to do this, but it bases its analysis on more sources than have ever been used before. Van der Lubbe claimed: 'I have been asked whether I carried this act out alone, and I declare that this was the case. Nobody helped me.'

During his speech to introduce the first German edition of the book in February 2008, just before the Reichtag fire's seventieth anniversary, Norbert Lammert, the current president of the German *Bundestag*, said: 'Whether this book will end the highly political dispute remains to be seen. However, it is certain that it offers an important contribution [to its resolution].' Frank Bajohr, a historian from Hamburg, phrased it similarly carefully: 'I hope Kellerhoff's book can end the controversy, but I doubt it.' He explained further: 'After all, his book shows that the subject has proved popular with conspiracy theorists and meddlers who have more than once exploited the media's sensationalist nature.'

Now, several years after the first edition was published in Germany, it is clear that both Lammert and Bajohr were right. Even though those who believe in the Nazis' guilt were unable to find fault with the book on factual grounds, they nonetheless demanded, by way of a string of lawsuits, that the book be taken off the shelves. However, their objection was based on just one accidently incorrectly referenced internet article. As they were unable to come up with substantial objections, they opted for insults and slander instead.

There is little value in such an approach. Those who avoid fact-led debates because they lack valid arguments ought to reconsider their hypothesis. But that is something conspiracy theorists never do. They simply repeat their arguments, perhaps packaged slightly differently, but mostly just more loudly and heatedly. However, this does not aid the advancement of knowledge in any way.

Perhaps the hope that, one day, serious historical scholarship will prevail in the debate about the Reichstag fire is misguided. This book cannot do more than to present the actual facts and explain the background to the debate since 1945. Unlike Hett's latest book, and many similar publications before his, this book remains objective at all times. None of the big questions remain unanswered, apart from one: why do Hett and his allies, to the present day, feel they 'have to' prove the Nazis' guilt?

To debunk the theory that it was the Nazis themselves who set the Reichstag on fire, a notion originally put forward by upstanding opponents of Hitler, does not change the historical facts of the Holocaust or the war of annihilation waged by the *Wehrmacht*. On the contrary, replacing false claims with indisputable facts is undoubtedly progress. It is not true that four million people were gassed or killed in other ways in Auschwitz-Birkenau, as was claimed for decades, even into the 1990s. The real number is 1.1 million or more, of which at least 900,000 were deported Jews. Although the figure is smaller, it does not make the monstrous genocide of the Jews a lesser crime.

Even seventy years after Hitler's suicide, it seems unlikely that the exhausting and nonsensical debate about the Reichstag fire – a case that has long been resolved – will come to an end in the near future. In Germany, it has been possible to check the conspiracy theorists' claims against the simple facts in this book since 2008. Now this will also be possible in the English language, thanks to publisher Michael Leventhal and translator Karina Berger. Those who categorically want to believe that the National Socialists were responsible for the Reichstag fire will not be convinced by this book. More important, however, are those who so far have not been able to engage with this subject in an unbiased manner. This is who this book is intended for.

Sven Felix Kellerhoff
Berlin
January 2016

INTRODUCTION

by Hans Mommsen

It remains to be seen whether this book will be able to end the
dispute about who set fire to the Reichstag, a dispute that has
now been going on for over eighty years. In his book, Sven Felix
Kellerhoff presents a straightforward and coherent account of the
complex sequence of events, as well as the subsequent discussion in the
press, which continues to this day. He comes to the conclusion that there
can be no doubt that Marinus van der Lubbe was the lone perpetrator.

Based on the careful analysis of available sources, Kellerhoff
charts the outbreak of the fire, the Reich Cabinet's reaction, the
political advantage Hitler gained from the event, the oppression of
the leftist opposition, the *Gleichschaltung* [co-ordination] that was
imposed immediately after the event and Hitler's first steps towards a
dictatorship. The author continues by describing the Reichstag fire's
far-reaching consequences for the success of National Socialism and
the almost instant dispute over who was responsible for the fire – the

communists or the National Socialists – and whether the confessed arsonist van der Lubbe had simply served as a straw man. The objective statements by the investigating police inspectors, which supported the theory of van der Lubbe having acted alone, were drowned out by the elaborate propaganda war.

The controversy about the Reichstag fire, outlined by Kellerhoff, survived the collapse of the Nazi regime and has not abated to this day. After 1945, few people doubted that the National Socialists were the culprits, although Hermann Göring had convincingly denied the charge at the International Military Tribunal in Nuremberg. Public opinion in general supported Hans-Bernd Gisevius' testimony and the description in his 1946 autobiography *Bis zum bitteren Ende* [*To the Bitter End*; republished in 2008 as *Valkyrie*]. Kellerhoff exposes these as myths manufactured by a cockalorum. They nonetheless formed the starting point of all later attempts to cast the blame on the National Socialists.

Kellerhoff also describes the way in which amateur historian Fritz Tobias brought about a clear break with the consensus regarding the Reichstag fire. Based on extensive research, Tobias proved in 1961 that van der Lubbe had told the truth and that the National Socialists had nothing to do with the arson attack. At first, few believed Tobias' thesis that van der Lubbe was the lone perpetrator. I had the same experience after I supported his thesis in a review of his book *Der Reichstagsbrand. Legende und Wirklichkeit* [*The Reichstag Fire. Legend and Reality*] in the *Stuttgarter Zeitung* on 5 July 1962. A solid phalanx of historians and interested *Zeitzeugen* [contemporary witnesses] launched a downright campaign against all those who believed in the theory of a lone perpetrator.

Kellerhoff guides his readers through the long-standing tale of the heroic struggle by a series of activists against the alleged 'legend of the Nazis' innocence'. First, Karl Dietrich Bracher dismissed Tobias as a scientific dilettante. Tobias had drawn his attention to the fact – politely, at first, then more bluntly – that Fire Chief Gempp, who had been portrayed as a Nazi victim by Bracher, had been found guilty of bribery by the superior court of justice in Berlin and had subsequently committed suicide. Ever since, Tobias had been accused of dilettantism, although his opponents did not object to allocating column space to authors with no professional qualifications in the prestigious academic journals *Historische Zeitschrift* and *Vierteljahreshefte*.

The methods used in the campaign against Tobias became increasingly unfair. Thus, Walther Hofer, a professor from Bern who spearheaded the campaign, had no qualms about denouncing Tobias to his superior, the Lower Saxon interior minister, for 'whitewashing' Hitler. There were many other cases of defamation, too. In 1968, the Croatian journalist Edouard Calic took advantage of the economic situation and founded the 'International Committee for Scholarly Research on the Causes and Consequences of the Second World War' in Luxembourg. For this, he secured the support of well-known names, as well as financial support from the Federal Press Office and the Federal Agency for Civic Education. This enabled him to pay visiting dignitaries lavish fees for their mere presence. Hofer supported these machinations and, as a result, got entangled in a net of forgeries that Calic fabricated in order to prove the Nazis' guilt.

This strategy – later continued by Alexander Bahar, Wilfried Kugel and Hersch Fischler – was ultimately bound to fail ignominiously. The credit for exposing the web of lies that Calic had spun, with Hofer's backing, is due in large part to Karl-Heinz Janßen, then senior editor at the weekly paper *Die Zeit*. However, those who believe that the Nazis are to blame have still not given up their fight against the alleged 'legend of the Nazis' innocence' – although this fight has increasingly become an end in itself. International research, meanwhile, has been getting back to business as usual and no longer doubts that van der Lubbe was the lone perpetrator.

Kellerhoff describes the debate – seemingly grotesque in hindsight – with cool detachment. As part of his critical examination, he also considers the role that radio and television broadcasters played in the campaign. The true scandal, which to this day has not been sufficiently acknowledged, lies in the failure of Germany's historians, not least the *Institut für Zeitgeschichte* [Institute for Contemporary History], which acted, again and again, as a crony to the forger-mafia, and was not afraid to back forgers.

The crucial reason why the controversy has been so fraught with emotion can be found in Bracher's allegation that his opponents 'trivialised' Hitler and National Socialism. This was reiterated when Hofer commented that a lone perpetrator would be 'pedagogically' undesirable for the 'German people'. As Kellerhoff emphasises, it is the predominant view of Hitler as a cynical, calculating, power-hungry politician who was in total control that lies behind the arson attack's 'potential to cause such tremendous agitation'. This point of view demonstrates the way in which the quasi-religious Hitler cult was retrospectively turned around and demonised. Kellerhoff rightly states that the insistence on the Nazis' guilt carries an exculpatory element, which casts 'the majority of Germans' as 'victims of a meticulous plan that was ruthlessly executed'. What is needed is a public inquiry into the political implications of the controversy surrounding the Reichstag fire. Kellerhoff's commendable analysis forms the basis for this.

Hans Mommsen

Feldafing

Sadly, Hans Mommsen passed away in 2015.

THE ARSON ATTACK

THE REICHSTAG ON FIRE – WAS THE CULPRIT CAUGHT IN THE ACT?

It was four to five degrees below zero in Berlin's city centre on the evening of 27 February 1933; an icy easterly wind made it seem even colder. In every other way, however, this appeared to be an ordinary winter evening. There was nothing to suggest that the events of this night would go down in German history and cause heated debates until the present day. An election campaign was taking place – the following Sunday, the Germans were to vote for yet another new parliament, even though barely six months had passed since the last election. And of course much had changed since Adolf Hitler had been appointed Reich chancellor exactly four weeks earlier, heading up a coalition of the *Nationalsozialistische Deutsche Arbeiterpartei* [NSDAP; National Socialist German Workers' Party] and the far-right *Deutschnationale Volkspartei* [DNVP; German National People's Party, usually known informally as the German Nationals or simply the Nationalists]. Since then, the publication of communist and social-democratic newspapers had not been permitted on several occasions. From 22 February onwards, thousands of SA and SS [*Schutzstaffel*; protection squadrons] men had been appointed as auxiliary policemen; a position many abused. Brawls between these gangs of Nazi 'brownshirts' and supporters of the *Rotfrontenkämpferbund* [Red Front Fighters' League] became increasingly common; in the capital alone, more than a dozen people had been killed as a result of these riots since 30 January. Nobody still believed that the parties taking part in the election campaign did so with equal chances. While the Prussian police force, controlled by Hermann Göring, would dissolve meetings of the opposition for trivial reasons, the NSDAP was practically never interfered with in this way.[1]

It was quiet in the Reichstag building on 27 February, as Reich President Paul von Hindenburg had dissolved parliament immediately after Hitler's appointment. The *Kommunistische Partei Deutschlands* [KPD; Communist Party of Germany] was using its offices in the building after its regular party headquarters, the Karl-Liebknecht-Haus at Bülowplatz, had recently been occupied, searched and closed by the police. However, Hitler's opponents were not yet giving up: the *Sozialdemokratische Partei Deutschlands* [SPD; Social Democratic Party of Germany] had brought forward the original date of its large convention at the Sportpalast to mark the fiftieth anniversary of Karl Marx's death from 14 March to this Monday evening in order to mobilise as many voters as possible. However, the police broke up the event, which led to concerns that an unauthorised demonstration by angry social democrats might take place in the government district. In the end, the crowd dispersed peacefully and the area around the Reichstag remained quiet.[2]

However, the calm only lasted until 9.00 p.m. It was at this time that theology student Hans Flöter was on his way home. He tried to work in the Prussian State Library as often as possible, and on this night too he had worked until late in the reading rooms of the magnificent building, located on the boulevard Unter den Linden. Now he was briskly walking home, turning into the Hindersinstraße between the Reichstag and the river Spree. He crossed the Königsplatz and walked past the Bismarck Memorial and the west side of the Reichstag, which was only sparsely lit – the Berlin magistrate had advised the municipal gas works to light only every other street lamp from 1 October 1932. Flöter was just crossing the southern end of the driveway of the parliament building when he was startled by the sharp sound of breaking glass. The noise came from the Reichstag building, or, to be exact, from a window on the main floor, right next to the large portico. The student looked up when he heard the noise again. Evidently, glass was being broken – and that was likely to be bad news. His suspicion was confirmed when he was able to make out a person who seemed to be carrying a burning object. Flöter had seen enough: this was a case for the police. As he walked past the Reichstag building regularly, he knew that two *Schupos* – as policemen were commonly known in Berlin – patrolled the area in the evenings. The student ran off straight away and indeed came across an officer, Chief Constable (Oberwachtmeister) Karl Buwert, on the northern side of the driveway. Flöter called out to him that someone had forcefully gained entry to the parliament building, but the policeman hesitated at first. It was only when the student told him that he had seen fire that Buwert reacted and ran to the other side of the driveway. Flöter felt he had fulfilled his civic duty and continued on his way home. Before he set off, he checked his watch: it was 9.05 p.m.[3]

Immediately afterwards, Buwert spotted flickering flames on the main floor. Two more pedestrians had approached the policeman by now. The 21-year-old typesetter Werner Thaler was on his way to the Lehrter train station on the other side of the river. When he passed the southern portal, he also heard the shattering of glass and thought he could make out two men on the balcony in front of the Reichstag restaurant – but it could also have been one man and his shadow. Right away, Thaler looked for someone to alert, and found Buwert. At about the same time, another man had come up to Buwert. At first, the policeman thought it was the student Flöter, but he had already continued towards the Spree river. The three men – Buwert, Thaler and the young man – now stared at the window of the Reichstag restaurant. Already, several curtains were aflame and there was no longer any doubt that they were witnessing an arson attack on the parliament building. Thaler shouted: 'Shoot!' The policeman grabbed his gun and aimed at the silhouette now moving through the ground floor of the south-western wing, but did not hit his target. Only seconds later, at around 9.10 p.m., Buwert told the young man: 'Run and raise the alarm at the Brandenburger Tor police station. Tell them that the Reichstag is on fire!' The young man did not hesitate and ran off towards the Pariser Platz square. Meanwhile, two couples had run up to the policeman to tell him they had spotted flames in the Reichstag building. Buwert sent them to raise the alarm as well. After the two men and one of the women had unsuccessfully searched for a fire alarm box, they went to the 'Haus der Ingenieure' ['House of Engineers'] in the Friedrich-Ebert Straße to ask the porter to alert the fire brigade by telephone. While Buwert continued to watch the flames behind the windows in the south-western wing of the Reichstag, he was joined by two colleagues who had been on patrol in the Tiergarten park and had been alarmed by the gun shot. After a brief discussion, one of them ran off towards the fire alarm box located in the Moltkestraße. It was 9.12 p.m.[4]

One minute later, the main fire station in Berlin's Lindenstraße received the emergency call from the 'Haus der Ingenieure'. The nearest fire station in Linienstraße 128/129 was notified immediately, and the first fire engine raced to the scene at 9.14 p.m.

The Berlin fire service sent more than sixty vehicles to the burning Reichstag. Firefighters from fifteen districts were at the scene. (National Archives, Washington DC)

Another fire engine left the station at Turmstraße 22 just sixty seconds later, when the alarm from the fire alarm box in the Moltkestraße was received. As the alarm had not been raised from within the Reichstag building itself, the mobilisation of a third fire station – the planned procedure in the event of a fire in parliament – did not take place. The four fire engines from each station drove towards the Reichstag

21

building sounding their bells and horns but, according to regulations, 'carefully enough to safely reach the destination'. At about the same time, the young man that Buwert had sent to raise the alarm arrived at the Brandenburger Tor police station. He called: 'Come straight away! The Reichstag building is on fire!' The duty officer, Police Lieutenant Emil Lateit, jumped up and got in the patrol car with two policemen; more men were to follow in a lorry. In accordance with the rules, one of the remaining officers noted their time of departure in the incident book: 9.15 p.m.

When Lateit arrived at the scene two minutes later, he immediately identified the situation as an emergency. He sent one of his assistants back to the police station to request reinforcement from police headquarters. Chief Constable Buwert reported to the lieutenant that the fire brigade had already been notified. Lateit gave the order to raise a major alarm and then ran off in order to find a way into the Reichstag. The southern portal was locked, and the porter's office unstaffed, so the 34-year-old police officer ran down the Sommerstraße along the east facade of the building, where two further doorways were located, but they were also locked. Lateit kept running until he finally came across the night porter, Albert Wendt, in the northern portal, which remained open until 10.00 p.m. The porter had only just heard about the fire from another policeman – this was understandable, as this porter's office was on the other side of the building, more than 100 metres away from the crime scene. Wendt promptly rang his boss, Maintenance Manager (Hausinspektor) Alexander Scranowitz, but was unable to reach him. Seconds later, the phone rang and the porter heard Scranowitz ask what was going on. The maintenance manager had seen the fire brigade race past his nearby riverside flat. Wendt told him that there was a fire in the restaurant of the Reichstag building. Scranowitz snapped: 'And you haven't reported this to me?' He grabbed his coat and rushed over to the parliament building. It was about 9.20 p.m. when Scranowitz arrived at the portal facing the Spree river, and he immediately went inside with several policemen. They walked quickly through a long hall – the so-called *Wandelhalle* – to assess the situation, but lost sight of each other. Lateit was the first to check the plenary chamber, probably around 9.21 p.m. He saw open flames around the president's table and felt the intense heat. The lieutenant turned around and ran back to the portal, noticing other small fires along the way. Lateit was convinced: this many individual fires could not have developed without someone's interference. He told his colleagues: 'Pistols out! Arson!', then returned to the station to file a report. Meanwhile, at around 9.23 p.m., the maintenance manager and policeman Helmut Poeschel also reached the parliament building's central room. Scranowitz glanced inside for 'only a split second' and then 'very quickly' closed the door again. In that short moment, however, he noticed that the curtains behind the wooden president's desk were already ablaze. So far, however, there was not much smoke in the vast room.[5]

At this point, the fire-fighting operations in the Reichstag building had just begun. At around 9.22 p.m., Senior Fire Chief (Oberbrandmeister) Emil Puhle and his men from the Linienstraße fire station reached the main floor via scaling ladders. Puhle single-handedly smashed one of the parliament restaurant's windows; in his haste, he did not notice that the adjoining window had already been broken into. The smaller fires in the restaurant were quickly put out, but because the firefighters did not know whether there were more fires further inside the building, Puhle kept going. At about the same time, Fire Chief Waldemar Klotz and his men from the Turmstraße fire station entered the Reichstag through the northern portal; they stormed onto the main floor with bucket pumps. While Klotz was stamping out some small flames in the carpet of one of the lobbies, he noticed a bright light ahead of him, towards the centre of the building. He had a look in the plenary chamber around 9.25 p.m., which was

The plenary chamber was destroyed. By cooling the fire, the firefighters tried to prevent it from spreading to other areas of the parliament building. (National Archives, Washington DC)

now dark and full of dense smoke. Although he could not see any open flames, he was suddenly hit by a wave of extraordinary heat. Instinctively, Klotz quickly closed the swing door again to prevent 'darting flames'. The fire chief knew what to do: he asked for a hose to cool down the plenary chamber with water. Even though it took

Klotz and his men just two minutes to get the hose ready, they were too late to prevent major damage.[6]

At around 9.27 p.m., according to the report that Berlin Fire Chief (Branddirektor) Gustav Wagner later filed, the plenary chamber 'suddenly turned into a sea of flames'. Back at the Reichstag, Senior Fire Chief Puhle noticed that when he opened the door to the chamber he was first hit by a wave of heat, but that the draught then abruptly pulled the other way. After that, he saw a roaring flame that shot 'up towards the cupola'. From one moment to the next, the plenary chamber had turned into 'a sea of flames – all the way around, from top to bottom, and in the middle', that emanated a 'great, blazing heat'. Fire Chief Klotz also watched the way the flames were rapidly spreading: 'I could see the room turning red from the flames through the frosted glass window, through which I was watching.' A further fire officer, Fritz Polchov, told the police that he had 'never experienced a draught like this at a fire' and that he 'literally had to hold on so as not to be pulled into the flames'. His colleague Willy König said he had been reminded of the 'flames of a forge'; he had also felt the sudden change of draught. Just moments later, the fire flared up with an 'audible pop'. One fire officer said it was as though 'a rocket had exploded'. Immediately after, the glass ceiling in the plenary chamber burst, giving the flickering flames access first to the air space beneath the cupola and, when its glass could no longer withstand the flames, to the cold February air outside. With the room's conditions now resembling those of a fireplace, the wooden interior of the plenary chamber was devoured by the flames.[7]

After checking the plenary chamber, Maintenance Manager Scranowitz and policeman Poeschel continued to search the main floor. They rushed through several adjoining rooms; the sound of their footsteps was swallowed by the thick carpets. Finally, they arrived in the Bismarck Hall. They were standing beneath the large chandelier when, around 9.26 p.m., they saw a figure stumbling towards them from the

A short break on the steps of the East Hall of the Reichstag turns into a photo opportunity. Numerous police officers were also at the scene. (National Archives, Washington DC)

southern inner courtyard, where the clubrooms were located. When the man spotted the two men, he stopped abruptly and then took a step back. However, Poeschel had already raised his gun and shouted: 'Hands up!' The figure, bare-chested except for braces, immediately raised his arms. Poeschel could now see that the man was a scruffy fellow, tall and burly, with dark, untidy hair that hung into his face. The policeman quickly searched the young man, but did not find any weapons, apart from a pocket knife, which he confiscated. In his back pocket he found a passport. There was no doubt: this man did not belong inside the parliament building, particularly not at the time

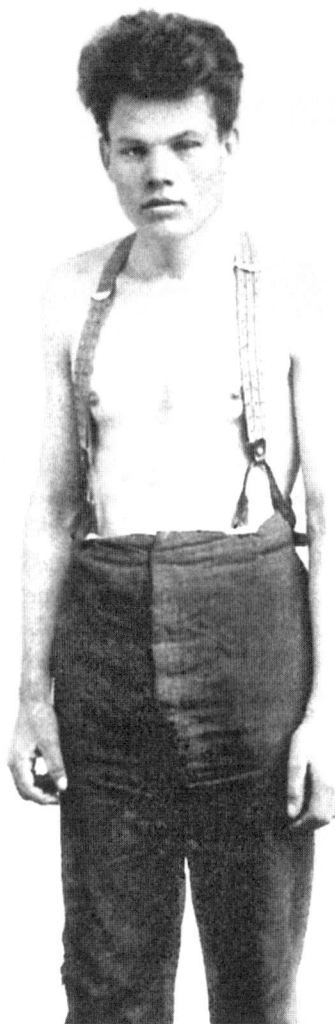

Marinus van der Lubbe was only wearing his trousers and braces when he was arrested. Reconstructed photograph, taken 28 February 1933. (Kellerhoff archive)

of a fire-fighting operation. Poeschel was sure he had apprehended the arsonist. Scranowitz, shaking with rage, shouted at the suspect: 'Why did you do this?' The heavily accented reply was: 'Protest, protest!' The maintenance manager was no longer able to control himself, and punched the man hard. Poeschel frogmarched the man – who, according to his passport, was a Dutchman called Marinus van der Lubbe – to the exit. There, someone threw a blanket over him, and Poeschel walked him over to the Brandenburger Tor police station. According to the log book, they arrived at 9.35 p.m.[8]

THE FIRE

FIRE-FIGHTING OPERATIONS, EYEWITNESSES AND FIRST REACTIONS BY NSDAP LEADERS

More than two dozen firemen and police officers were in the Reichstag building when, just before 9.30 p.m., the relatively contained flames in the plenary chamber suddenly turned into a fire of catastrophic proportions. After their initial shock, several of the men recognised the gravity of the situation and, independently of one another, gave the order to raise the alarm level. For this, however, a fire alarm box or telephone needed to be found, as firemen did not yet carry radios. The main fire station in Kreuzberg received several requests for back-up between 9.31 p.m. and 9.33 p.m., and immediately contacted additional fire stations. One and a half minutes later, a further three dozen fire engines were on their way. After alerting the fire stations, a call was made to Berlin's Fire Chief Walter Gempp. He was picked up by car and brought to the Reichstag as soon as possible, where he arrived around 9.41 p.m. Just one minute later, the fire chief sounded a major alarm. Another five fire stations sent out fire engines, and several fire boats were already making their way up the river Spree. By now, almost all of Berlin's fire services were at the scene – from the fire station in the Suarezstraße in west Berlin to the Lichtenberg fire station in the east; from Wedding in the north to Steglitz in the south. An eyewitness commented that the firemen did their 'difficult job' while remaining 'remarkably calm and organised'.[9]

The fire reached its peak around 9.45 p.m. A reporter from the newspaper *Berliner Tageblatt* reported: 'Surrounded by the four side wings, the huge glass cupola, illuminated by the flaming fire, towers into the night sky. The glow of the flames, blazing away on the inside, lights up the surrounding dark parts of the building. The flames are licking at the cupola's stone lantern.' The journalist was on the phone, dictating his impressions to the editorial office in the Jerusalemer Straße, which printed his words almost verbatim in the morning edition:

> Sparks are flying through the air and are carried across the square in front of the Reichstag building by the strong winds. There is no sign of the fire deeper inside the building on the lower floors, which are visible from the street. The red glow of the fire is only visible from the Sommerstraße, where the light from the flames lights up the large coloured windows in the stairwell.[10]

By the time the dome was brightly lit by the flames, it was possible to see, even from a few streets away, that something was wrong in the parliament building. When schoolboy Reinhold Thielitz, who lived in the Hindersinstraße with his parents, heard the news from his mother, he rushed to the window:

> At this point, the dome was still intact, and brightly lit by the flames. I called Ullstein [publishing house] immediately to report the fire. In those days

one was paid three or five marks for that. As far as I can remember, I was the second caller. Then I ran outside. It was a cold, dark and stormy night.

According to the newspaper *Vossische Zeitung*, 'many other residents came running as soon as they heard: "The Reichstag is on fire."' Soon the crowd swelled to 'several thousand' and, at around 9.40 p.m., the police had to set up barriers to 'control the crowds'. There was much to see for the onlookers, as a journalist for the daily newspaper *Berliner Lokalanzeiger*, who had rushed to the scene, reported: 'Enormous flames shot out of the dome, which were visible even from Charlottenburg and the city centre.' The daily newspaper *Berliner Morgenpost* reported:

> On all sides, the Reichstag building resembles an occupied fort. It is surrounded by endless rows of fire engines, red hose lines, and mountains of ladders, which are of no use at the moment as the fire is raging mainly on the inside and up towards the dome. On all four fronts, firemen have smashed the windows of the building and hose lines are being rolled inside.

The journalist also noted the 'incredible crowds' surrounding the building, as well as the barriers. Only ministers and MPs were being admitted now, 'with Göring, the president of the Reichstag, leading the way'.

However, the reporter of the *Morgenpost*, keen to get inside, also managed to get access to the burning building. He reported:

> Inside, the damage is striking. The large halls are filled with smoke, and policemen and firemen are frantically rushing around. Every single person who manages to access the building is subject to thorough identity checks: this is for good reason, as it was arson that caused the fire. Hose lines are being dragged across the red velour runners on the stairs and in the *Wandelhallen*; coming up the stairs one can already feel the incredible

heat blazing inside. The heat increases the closer one gets to the plenary chamber. It is impossible for anyone to enter the plenary chamber, even for the firemen in their protective gear – the red wall of flames is impassable. I got a glimpse of the sea of flames through the doors through which MPs normally walk in and out.

The firemen did their best, spraying tons of water into the fire. By this point it had become clear that the chamber itself was lost – now the main aim was to prevent the fire from spreading to further rooms in the building, especially the famous Reichstag library. There was also the risk that the solid stone pillars that supported the cupola would become unstable, which would put the entire building at risk.[11]

That evening, André François-Poncet, the French ambassador in Berlin, was having dinner with a large number of guests in the embassy's dining room at Pariser Platz, among them Lutz Schwerin von Krosigk, the reactionary finance minister in Hitler's Cabinet. Suddenly, a member of staff informed the host that the Reichstag building was on fire – according to François-Poncet's memory, this was around 9.00 p.m., though in reality it was at least half an hour later. The diplomat got up and went to an adjacent room from which it was possible to see, beyond the embassy's garden, the Reichstag's cupola in the near distance. He described the view in his memoirs: 'The glass cupola is bright red, as though illuminated by a red Bengal fire from the inside.' François-Poncet returned to his guests and passed on the news; he noted 'a look of surprise on all faces'. Only Schwerin von Krosigk is said to have cried out 'Thank God!' with 'strange delight'. It is more likely, however, that the Frenchman misheard him and that the finance minister had in fact said, 'Oh God!'[12]

At this time, Ernst Hanfstaengl, the foreign press chief of the Nazi party, was in bed with a high temperature. He was staying at the Palais, just opposite the Reichstag's east facade. Hanfstaengl had asked Göring

This press photograph shows the fire on 27 February 1933 around 10.00 p.m.
The cupola is illuminated by the fire in the plenary chamber; the other
windows by the light that had been switched on. (National Archives,
Washington DC)

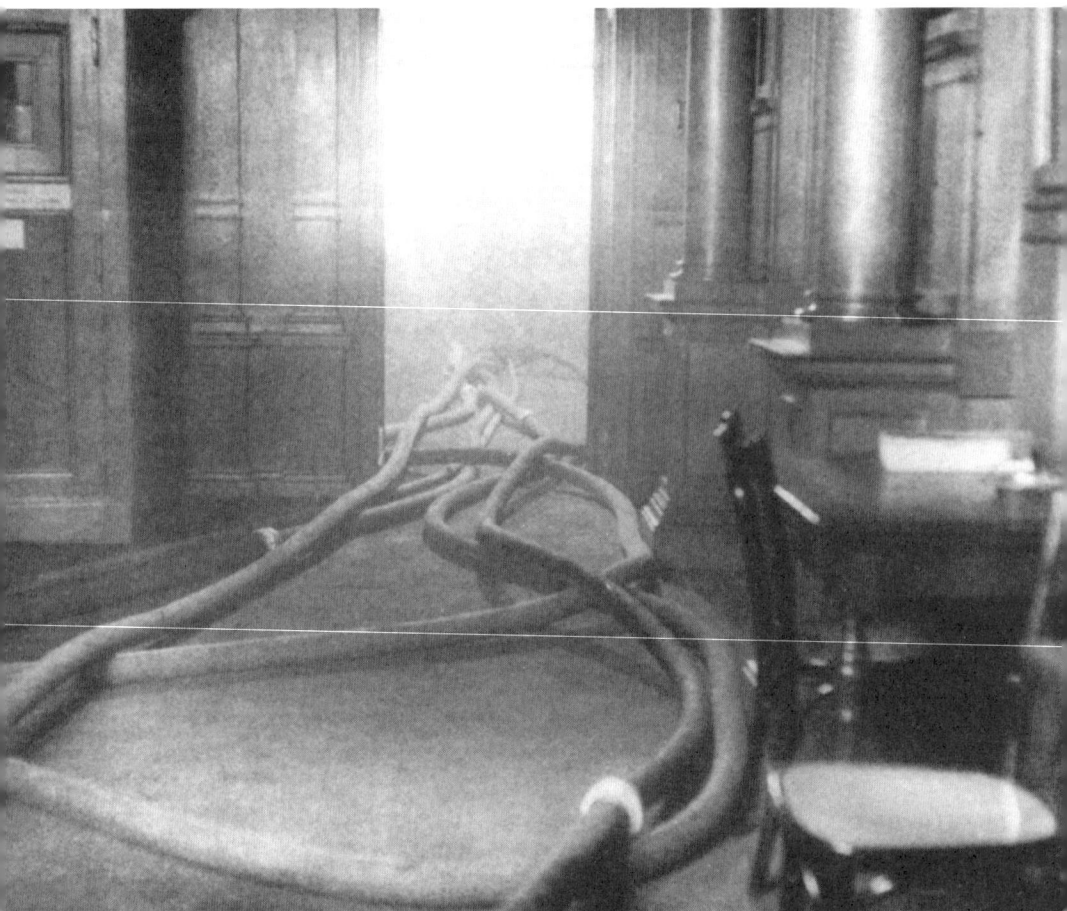

The journalist at the *Berliner Morgenpost* wrote: 'The hose lines roll into the building in a concentric fashion.' This photograph shows the club rooms near the plenary chamber. (National Archives, Washington DC)

for this arrangement in order to reduce 'Hitler's hotel costs'; it also 'didn't cost Göring a penny' as he never used his official residence at the Palais. Because he was unwell, Hanfstaengl had cancelled an invitation to Joseph Goebbels' flat in Charlottenburg on 27 February – he had been meant to play the grand piano for Hitler – and had gone to bed early. Suddenly he awoke with a start, as his room was ablaze with light. Before he was entirely awake, a member of staff rushed into his room and cried: 'Sir, Sir, the Reichstag is on fire!' Hanfstaengl immediately jumped out of bed and ran to the window, probably only a few minutes after 9.30 p.m. He ran to the telephone:

> I called Goebbels. 'I must speak to Mr Hitler,' I said, breathlessly. Goebbels asked what the matter was, and whether he could pass on a message. Impatiently, I said: 'Tell him the Reichstag building is on fire!' – 'Hanfstaengl, is that meant to be a joke?' Goebbels asked curtly. 'If you believe I would make a joke like that, then come here and see for yourself,' I replied, and hung up.

Annoyed, Hanfstaengl next informed several foreign correspondents. When he put down the phone, it rang. It was Goebbels, calling back to find out what was really going on. However, the foreign press chief, who was not on good terms with the Berlin *Gauleiter* [NSDAP district leader], brushed him off: 'Come here and find out for yourself whether I'm talking nonsense or not. The entire building is on fire and the fire brigade is already here.' Only a few hours later, Goebbels noted in his diary: 'Hitler and Auwi [Prince August Wilhelm von Preußen] come at 9.00 p.m. Music and chitchat. Then phone call from Hanfstaengl: The Reichstag building is on fire; ridiculous. But he's right. Hitler and I race down there straight away.' Goebbels' flat at the Reichskanzlerplatz was about 8km away from the Reichstag, so the NSDAP leader and his chief propagandist, as well as an accompanying car, arrived at least twenty minutes after the second telephone call with Hanfstaengl, probably just after 10.00 p.m.[13]

For Hermann Göring it was less of a journey. Göring had by now accumulated several posts in questionable fashion: he was simultaneously president of the Reichstag, a minister without portfolio in the Cabinet, acting commissar for the Prussian ministry of the interior and Reich minister for aviation. He was spending this evening in his most important office, the Prussian ministry of the interior at Unter den Linden 72/73, between Wilhelmstraße and Shadowstraße. According to the National Socialist press, he was planning to 'muck out' Prussia, the country's biggest state that comprised three-fifths of Germany's surface area, inhabitants and police force, in this last week before the Reichstag elections. Göring himself phrased it ostensibly more harmlessly: 'I expect and hope that all civil servants will unite with me behind the goal to save the Fatherland from the threat of decline by strengthening and pooling all national forces.' Göring's office received news of the fire between 9.20 p.m. and 9.25 p.m. It is unclear when exactly it was received, and by whom, as several people later claimed to have passed on the message, including a porter at the Palais and the Maintenance Manager Scranowitz, who had asked his wife to inform the president. An adjutant interrupted Göring's discussion with Ludwig Grauert, the recently appointed head of the police division of the ministry. According to his memory, his boss had said: 'This is a huge mess. Get me a car, I'm going straight away!' At around this time, the fire in the plenary chamber suddenly started to spread. At about 9.45 p.m., Göring's limousine arrived at the Reichstag and he entered the building. Douglas Reed, the Berlin correspondent of *The Times*, managed to surreptitiously join his entourage:

> I ran across the street and arrived at portal II, the MPs' entrance, just as a large man in a huge trench coat and soft hat appeared in front of me and entered the building with a few others. I followed them. Inside, there were one or two policemen, and firemen were carrying in a hose. The man in the trench coat appeared determined, and was very angry. He spotted a man making a telephone call in a phone box near the entrance. He ran up to him and angrily asked him what he thought he was doing there. The man,

a journalist who had been talking to his editorial office, experienced a very uncomfortable thirty seconds before he was able to explain his presence. The large man told him to leave.

It was never discovered which newspaper the journalist worked for, although it is clear that at least two reporters – one of the *Berliner Morgenpost* and one of the *Lokalanzeiger* – had accessed the Reichstag before the official press conference took place. It may have been one of these two that Göring threw out. When, soon after, the president of the Reichstag noticed an unknown man in his entourage, Douglas Reed was also forced to leave the building immediately. The message was unequivocal: 'The press is not welcome here.'[14]

A few minutes later, Fire Chief Gempp gave Göring an update. According to Gempp, this conversation took place 'around a quarter of an hour after I arrived'. Of course, the fire chief had already had a look around: 'I had been into the building by then. The plenary chamber was ablaze. Before I left the room, I gave my men the order to withdraw a little, as there was a risk of the building collapsing.' Indeed, it was very dangerous beneath the cupola: 'The fire-fighting operations were turning out to be very difficult. The firemen were unable to enter the chamber, as burnt pieces of wood panelling and iron parts kept crashing to the ground.' After telling his men to withdraw, Gempp left the chamber to give orders to the other rescue units. On his way, he encountered Göring. After Gempp had duly reported to Göring, he was told: 'Don't mind me. You're in charge.' By now it would have been almost 10.00 p.m.[15]

Shortly afterwards, Hitler arrived at the Reichstag building with Goebbels. Goebbels' first impression was: 'The entire building is on fire.' Just as Reed had tried when Göring entered the building, another British journalist now attempted to join the chancellor and his companion on their way in. Sefton Delmer, the correspondent for the *Daily Express*, had been in his flat between Potsdamer Platz and Landwehrkanal when he heard about the fire. As his car was parked a long way away in a garage and he was unable to get a taxi, he ran the entire way – more than 2km – to the Reichstag. He walked around

Hitler's inner circle in February 1933 (from left): Press Chief Otto Dietrich, Foreign Press Chief Ernst 'Putzi' Hanfstaengl, Hermann Göring, Hitler, SA Chief of Staff Ernst Röhm, Reich Minister of the Interior Wilhelm Frick. (Kellerhoff archive)

the burning building and spoke to a few eyewitnesses, including his colleague Douglas Reed, who told him about what had happened with Göring. "'Oh God, how embarrassing," I thought. "Beaten by *The Times*, that boring old stagecoach. How terrible!"' But just then, Delmer noticed that Hitler had arrived and was about to rush into the building. Cheekily, Delmer enquired whether he might go with him. He was allowed to join and filed his report that same night. The next day, the *Daily Express* came out with the exclusive headline: 'The Reichstag in Flames Last Night. *Daily Express* Correspondent Accompanies Hitler into Blazing Building.'

In one of the chambers, Hitler's group came across Göring. According to the *Daily Express*, Göring said straight away: 'There is no doubt that this was caused by communists, Mr Chancellor. Several communist MPs were here in the building, just twenty minutes before the fire started. We have arrested one of the arsonists.' The president of the Reichstag, already the second most important person in the party at that time, pointed to the supposed evidence for arson: 'Here you can see, Mr Chancellor, how they started the fire: they draped items of clothing that had been soaked in petrol over the furniture and set them on fire.' By now the group had arrived at the plenary chamber on the main floor. Firemen were pointing their hoses through the open doors. Hitler walked up to them and had a look at the inferno inside. Then he turned around and said a few sentences, which Sefton Delmer recorded as such:

> This is a sign from God. If this fire turns out to have been caused by communists, as I believe is the case, then nothing will be able to stop us from wiping out this murderous pest with an iron fist. God grant that this be the work of the communists. You are now witnessing the beginning of a great new epoch in German history. This fire is just the beginning. You see this burning building. If the communist spirit takes hold of Europe

for even just two months, everything will be destroyed by fire, just like this building!

Another witness remembered Hitler's remark differently. Rudolf Diels, who had been head of the Prussian political police in Berlin for the past six months, had joined the small group looking into the plenary chamber. Göring saw him and, according to Diels, had immediately given clear instructions: 'This is the beginning of the communist revolt. Now they will attack! There's no time to lose!' At that moment, Hitler had turned around and, with a 'bright red' face, snorted and said:

> There will be no mercy. Anyone who stands in our way will be crushed. The German people will not support leniency. Each communist official we come across shall be shot. All communist MPs must be hanged tonight. Everyone associated with the communists must be arrested. Social democrats and the *Reichsbanner* [umbrella organisational flag for all social democratic-dominated paramilitary forces during the Weimar Republic] will also no longer be spared.

At the Prussian interior ministry, Diels had been engaged in the 'fight against the communist movement' since 1930. On his way to the Reichstag, he had stopped at the Brandenburger Tor police station to take a look at the arrested suspect. According to his later memoirs, Diels had told the chancellor that in his opinion the arsonist was 'crazy'. However, Hitler had interrupted him abruptly: 'This is a sophisticated crime that has been carefully planned. A nice idea by these criminals. But, my dear party comrades, they didn't reckon with us, did they!'[16]

Then the chancellor, the president of the Reichstag and a few others withdrew to a room unaffected by the fire to continue their conversation. Rudolf Diels meanwhile gave the necessary orders to an employee, who rang police headquarters straight away:

Minister Göring has raised a major alarm with the entire Prussian police force. I have already passed on the alert on police radio Karlshorst. Alert the division straight away. Everyone is to come to headquarters as soon as possible. The chief will be here shortly, and will be bringing the perpetrator. Make sure you are ready. You are to question the fellow straight away!

Hitler and his entourage enter the burning Reichstag shortly after 10.00 p.m. To the right, seen in profile, is the Reich chancellor; to the left, partly concealed, are Joseph Goebbels (light hat) and Hermann Göring (dark hat). (National Archives, Washington DC)

Diels went to the Brandenburger Tor police station to pick up Marinus van der Lubbe, who had been arrested on suspicion of arson, and drove him to the Alexanderplatz, where they arrived at 10.30 p.m.[17]

Around this time, several journalists were filing reports to their editorial offices. These were inserted next to the already typeset articles, so that the *Morgenpost* as well as the *Tageblatt* and the *Vossische Zeitung* all published several reports from different points in time alongside each other in their morning editions. The *Morgenpost* and Alfred Hugenberg's *Lokalanzeiger* even printed photographs of the fire-fighting operations in the burning Reichstag. However, following Göring's order to keep the press out of the building, all journalists were now waiting outside. The *Morgenpost* reported, not entirely accurately: 'By half past ten, the entire plenary chamber, including the seats and panelling of the president's desk, are already completely burned-out.' In reality, however, it was only now that the firefighters were beginning to gain some control over the flames. The reporter for the *Tageblatt* wrote: 'Now, around half past ten, the glow of the flames is growing darker. The cupola, which a short while ago was still glowing bright red, now only emanates a dark reflection of the fire, which continues to rage on further on the inside.' It was still too early for the all-clear, however: 'Even now the fire-fighting teams are unable to enter the centre of the plenary chamber, as the building is still in danger of collapsing. Lots of water is still being pumped into the room.' According to the article, it was not until about 11.00 p.m. that the 'fire's force' was contained. The fire brigade, in agreement with this assessment, now loosened the access restrictions for the press:

Shortly after 11 p.m., several journalists are given access to the building. They are able to observe the fire as part of an official guided tour. It is not possible to get to the original source of the fire, the plenary chamber – this part of the building is completely dark and is only illuminated by the firemen's torches and electric lamps.

BERLINER MORGENPOST

Wöchentlich 50 Pfennig

Nr. 50 — Dienstag, 28. Februar 1933 — 10 Pfennig

Brandstiftung:
Reichstags-Gebäude in Flammen

Innenraum bis zur Kuppel vernichtet.
Brandstifter verhaftet und geständig:
Ein holländischer Kommunist.

Der brennende Reichstag

The *Berliner Morgenpost*, Germany's newspaper with the highest circulation at the time, clearly distanced itself from the Prussian government's official statement. The headline 'Brandstiftung: Reichstags-Gebäude in Flammen' ['Arson Attack: Reichstag Building in Flames'] was matter-of-fact and only appeared on page two. The newspaper, published by the German-Jewish publisher Ullstein, was 'co-ordinated' just weeks later. (Kellerhoff archive)

By the time the fire had been extinguished, the rooms surrounding the plenary chamber were completely destroyed. Police officers supervised the firefighters' initial investigation. (Kellerhoff archive)

In addition, the journalist for the *Vossische Zeitung* reported that 'the fire started at several locations. It can be assumed without doubt that this was arson; it has just not yet been determined how it was carried out.' The several hundred firefighters managed to bring the fire under control just before midnight, although the plenary chamber, parts of the *Wandelhallen* and a few other rooms were still on fire. Thirteen fire brigades were on site. According to the *Tageblatt*, the process of 'dampening down the fire was also extraordinarily complicated, as the gold-plated domed structure on the large glass ceiling was in danger of collapsing'. After more than three hours of hard work, at around 1.00 a.m., most of the firefighters were relieved, yet it took the entire night and the following day to clear up. At this point, nobody could anticipate the consequences that the arson attack on the Reichstag would have.[18]

3

THE CONFESSION

MARINUS VAN DER LUBBE – AN ARSONIST'S BIOGRAPHY

Marinus van der Lubbe had cried 'protest! protest!' when, shortly after his arrest, he was asked why he had started the fire. Until the end of his life, the young Dutchman did not change this initial statement: 'I have been asked whether I carried out this act alone, and I declare that this was the case. Nobody helped me and I did not encounter a single person in the building.' Over the following months, the arsonist repeated the same statement, without major discrepancies. Those details of his statement that could be verified proved to be unusually precise. Essentially, all of the suspect's minuted testimonies were consistent with each other and with the results from on-site inspections. Van der Lubbe's statement was also unequivocal when questioned by the psychological experts Karl Bonhoeffer and Jürg Zutt: 'He denied from the beginning, and all the way through, that anyone else was involved. He said that he had planned it on his own, and had carried it out alone.'[19]

The youngest child of grocer Franciscus Cornelis van der Lubbe, Marinus van der Lubbe was born in 's-Hertogenbosch in 1909. His parents separated when he was young, and his mother looked after the seven children by herself until she died in 1921. Despite the difficult circumstances, van der Lubbe attended primary school, and then the Christian school in nearby Leiden for eighteen months. At the age of 12, he was taken in by one of his step-sisters and her husband, and began an apprenticeship as a bricklayer. He also attended evening classes. He was intelligent and curious, and borrowed a variety of books from the public library in Leiden, ranging from books by Henry Ford to *Das Kapital* by Karl Marx and travel literature by Sven Hedin. Influenced by his colleagues, van der Lubbe developed a worldview based on communist and anarchist ideas. His eyesight was irreparably damaged when lime powder got into his eyes during a tussle with other apprentices in 1926, and again during an accident at work eighteen months later. His visual impairment was so significant that he was unable to continue working as a builder. He was only able to secure occasional labouring work, but was occupied with more or less sensible political actions most of the time. His main enemy was the social welfare system, despite (or because of) the fact that he lived on disability benefits. However, he only received a meagre payment of 6.44 gilders, whereas he had earned a weekly salary of 26 gilders before his accident: 'Aged 19, he was half blind and destitute.'

Political activism became van der Lubbe's *raison d'être*. He joined the communist youth organisation 'De Zaaier' in 1927 and, two years later, the Dutch communist party's board in Leiden offered him the leadership of the local 'De Zaaier' group. Van der Lubbe dedicated all his time to his new role: he organised a club room and produced flyers, which he viewed as his newspaper and called 'De roode Arbeider'. He became a well-known activist in Leiden, but when, in 1931, he offered to run a campaign for communist-minded teenagers in Amsterdam, the communist party rejected his offer. Soon after, Marinus began his long journey through central Europe. It was his dream to make it to Bolshevist Russia, considered paradise by communists at the time. He made it to Berlin, but then gave up and turned back. After his return, he decided to attempt to swim across the North Sea – the prize for the first Dutchman to achieve this was set at 5,000 gilders. However, he abandoned this plan as well and began a new journey, this time to China. Along his way, which led him all the way to Yugoslavia and back, he attracted the attention of the police in several countries; he was briefly imprisoned a few times for not paying the bill and similar crimes. At the beginning of 1932, he fell out with the welfare centre in Leiden and smashed three of the building's windows. He was sentenced to three months in prison as a result. Yet before he was locked up, he took off travelling again, across Germany and Poland, all the way up to the Russian border. Here, though, he was arrested and deported to his home country, where he had to serve his sentence after all. Once he was released, Marinus van der Lubbe published another flyer declaring his views: 'Those unemployed who are willing to fight have become listless and uncertain. This has to stop […] So let's move forward, and take action ourselves!' Around the turn of the year 1932/33, the Dutchman came up with the idea of shooting and killing Adolf Hitler. However, a friend warned him that he would not be able to manage that with his bad eyesight. The conversation is said to have moved on to the idea of planting a bomb in the Berlin Reichstag, yet van der Lubbe did not pursue this any further.[20]

At the end of 1933, he realised that the political situation in neighbouring Germany was heating up. 'In the Netherlands, I read that the National Socialists had now come to power in Germany,' he said during an interrogation on 2 March 1933. He added: 'I have noticed that supporters of the government of National Concentration [Hitler's government] enjoy full freedom in Germany, but that workers do not. However, the labour movement is not the right force to motivate

Marinus van der Lubbe. The photographs were taken by the criminal investigation department and released shortly after. (National Archives, Washington DC)

workers to fight for freedom.' When, on 3 February, Chancellor Hitler announced to the generals of the *Reichswehr* [armed forces of the Weimar Republic] that he intended to destroy Marxism 'root and branch', van der Lubbe took off again. He arrived at his destination, Berlin, on 18 February. In the capital, he looked for workers with a revolutionary spirit, but without much success:

> I have realised that the workers will not take action of their own accord. Right now, just before the elections, the workers won't be willing to rise up, of their own accord, against a system in which one side enjoys freedom, and the other side suffers oppression. It was my opinion that something had to be done to protest against this system. As the workers didn't want to take action, I decided to do something. I thought some sort of arson attack would be good. I didn't want to target private citizens, but something that belonged to the system. I thought public buildings were a suitable target.

The young Dutchman made this decision in the evening of 25 February 1933.[21]

The Reichstag was not the first but the fourth building that van der Lubbe attempted to set on fire. Two days before he broke into the parliament building, he had experimented with arson on a shed belonging to the Neukölln welfare centre. He had gone there several times in the previous few days to meet and talk to like-minded Germans; he had assumed that these were most likely to be found among the unemployed picking up their meagre benefits. If we are to believe the indictment, a conversation about arson attacks as a political signal took place between a few supporters of the communist party and van der Lubbe. However, this account is based solely on the testimony of one witness, who seems to have been interested primarily in the promise of a reward. The Dutchman himself denies having been influenced in his decision by others: 'I can only repeat that I did not hear the conversation about setting fire to public buildings. When I had the idea to set fire to public buildings, I first thought of the Neukölln welfare centre, as it seemed to be the most suitable target.' Van der Lubbe began to prepare for the attack: visiting three different shops, he bought matches and four packs of firelighters branded 'Oldin' and 'Feuerfee'. The cubed blocks, of which there were two in each pack, were made of a mixture of sawdust and naphthalic acid. They ignited quickly and reliably, burned very hot and were therefore suitable for lighting fires in ovens. The sales assistants in the three shops remembered van der Lubbe.

Thus equipped, he arrived at the welfare centre in the Mittelstraße in Neukölln on Saturday afternoon, but it was still too light outside. Two and a half hours later, when the sun had gone down, he set to work. He threw half a block of firelighters through an open window, but it landed in the ladies' toilet, which had a fire-proof concrete floor; the lighters burned down without causing a fire. Van der Lubbe lit two more halves and threw them onto the shed's roof. However, the roofing felt took a long time to light, as there was still some snow on the roof.

When, finally, some flames appeared, they were noticed by a passer-by who alerted the police. The damage was insignificant.[22]

Van der Lubbe quickly left the crime scene and took the underground to Alexanderplatz in the city centre. His second target was the Red City Hall, where the mayor of Berlin was based, as this was a 'building representing the system': 'I saw that one of the basement windows was open at the corner [of Jüdenstraße and Rathausstraße]. I lit another pack of firelighters and threw them into the basement. It was already dark and nobody saw me.' Again, the arson attack failed, although this time it was a close call. It was not until an hour and a half later that Richard Kiekbusch, a stoker at the City Hall who lived in the basement flat, noticed the smell of burning and extinguished the fire with a few buckets of water. There was a hole in the floor the size of two palms, and the carpet and the base of a coat rack had also caught fire. The flames could have easily spread to the next room or – even more dangerously – to the store room on the other side, in which 'flammable substances' were kept, especially cleaning products and packing materials. However, Kiekbusch did not report the fire as he assumed it had been caused by negligence.[23]

Van der Lubbe quickly left the vicinity of the City Hall and carried on walking, this time towards the Berliner Schloss [Berlin Palace]. The magnificent, baroque building was to be his third target because 'it was situated in the city centre and the fire would have been visible for miles'. He added:

> I crossed the bridge over the river Spree, and then turned left and walked across the empty square. There is a big monument on one side of the castle. Building work was taking place on that side at the time, and there was lots of scaffolding. I climbed up to the left of the archway, and onto the roof.

The Dutchman looked for an open window into which he could throw his firelighters. 'I threw one packet into one of the skylights, but didn't wait to see whether it ignited.' This time, van der Lubbe almost caused a serious fire: the lighters set the window frame on fire. This could have had dangerous consequences had the fire spread to the dry wood of the ancient roof structure. However, one of the castle's firewardens happened to walk past on his rounds, spotted the fire and was able to extinguish it in time. The fire was reported in several newspapers.[24]

The three arson attacks had failed. Disappointed, van der Lubbe began his long walk home to the Netherlands. On Sunday, he walked to Hennigsdorf, a Berlin suburb. Yet that night, he changed his mind and decided to try to galvanise the German workers one last time. The Reichstag building was his new target, as this was the 'system's central point'. So, from Henningsdorf in the north-west, he marched back to the city centre. On his way, he bought four more packets of firelighters in Wedding. He arrived at the parliament building at around 2.00 p.m. and had a thorough look around. He was noticed by an employee, who later recalled the young man's 'awful appearance' and that he had looked 'like a tramp'. Like the previous Saturday, it was still too light outside. He waited a few hours and then returned to the Reichstag just after 8.30 p.m. He had found the perfect spot that afternoon: a corner of the building's west facade, just south of the portico. Despite the barbed wire, it was easy enough to climb the 4.5 metres to the main floor, holding and stepping onto the joints of the ground floor. This position had a further advantage: 'I chose this angle near the steps so that I wouldn't be seen entering the building from the street.' The nearest street lamp, which was only dimly lit, was 36.5 metres away. Just after 9.00 p.m., van der Lubbe was standing on the small balcony in front of the window, which he smashed 'with around ten kicks'. Armed with burning firelighters, he then climbed through the window and into the Reichstag restaurant.[25]

The arson department of the Berlin police had a photograph taken of the point of entry. The joints in the stone wall are clearly visible. The police found climbing marks on the wall. (Private collection)

Van der Lubbe gave a detailed description of the route he had taken through the Reichstag – first from memory and then, after the first visit to the scene on the afternoon of 28 February 1933, again in more detail. He was able to identify almost every spot where he had started a fire. He had also run down the stairs from the restaurant to the ground floor and had set alight several items, mainly serviettes and table cloths. However, this detour had been ineffective, as the rooms located on the ground floor contained mainly simple furniture and had walls that were partly tiled, which burned badly or not at all. Therefore, he ran back to the main floor and started more fires with paper and his last firelighters. When these had run out, he also used his coat and waistcoat, and finally his shirt, as torches to set alight anything that seemed flammable. At last, coming from the east side of the building, he reached the plenary chamber, where he set fire to the door curtains by the entrance and the president's desk:

> Through the flames of the burning heavy curtains I saw a large domed room that looked like a church. The desks were lower at the front, and higher at the back … It only took a few moments for the curtains outside the plenary chamber to burst into flames; the wood caught fire too, but burned more slowly.

In the adjoining rooms, van der Lubbe set fire to several sofas, armchairs and curtains before he hurried on, until he finally ran into Scranowitz and Poeschel in the Bismarck hall. According to the detailed investigation, it was estimated that this route, through roughly half of the parliamentary building, should have taken no more than fifteen minutes – enough time for van der Lubbe to set numerous fires.[26]

Of this, the two police inspectors in charge, Helmut Heisig and Walter Zirpins of the political police, were also convinced. In the final report on 3 March 1933, Zirpins stated: 'The question whether van der Lubbe carried this act out alone can be confirmed without hesitation. The investigation, the factual findings and the offender's detailed testimony substantiate this claim. Several additional leads emerged during the investigation, but these could not be verified.' Zirpins justified his view thus:

> Van der Lubbe gave a convincing description of the scene of the crime and the way it was carried out – with all the details, including sources of fire, the damage caused and the route he took. He did this from memory from the first time we questioned him, before he returned to the scene of the crime as part of the investigation. Only the person who carried the act out himself is capable of that. Nobody else would have been able to describe all of this in advance, especially the planned smaller fires, and then demonstrate it at the crime scene later.

An unknown superior in the Prussian police force, identifiable by the blue coloured pencil, placed a question mark next to these remarks.[27]

$$4$$

THE CONSEQUENCES

THE HUNT FOR COMMUNISTS, THE REICHSTAG FIRE DECREE AND THE ENABLING ACT

ermann Göring and Adolf Hitler were in immediate agreement that it was necessary to take drastic action against the communists. They had two meetings that night: the first took place between 10.30 p.m. and 11.00 p.m. in the president of the Reichstag's office in the parliament building, which was unaffected by the fire, and the second, soon after midnight, in Göring's office in the Prussian interior ministry at Unter den Linden 72/73. In these meetings, the new government's two most important men decided what should be done. Göring had already put the Prussian police force on standby before Hitler arrived; now he issued concrete orders. During the first meeting, the chancellor shouted and ranted. Rudolf Diels told a confidant that Hitler had 'vilified the communist subhumans' in a 'seemingly never-ending choleric outburst'. He added that for Hitler 'there was no need for even a semblance of evidence that the communists had wanted to proclaim the beginning of their boastfully announced mass action with this disgraceful arson attack on a German palladium'. As a result of this choleric fit, he demanded all communist MPs to be hanged immediately. However, Hitler's government could not (yet) afford to act so boldly. Further witnesses of his outburst were Reich Minister of the Interior Wilhelm Frick, Berlin's Police Chief Magnus von Levetzow and Goebbels, who later noted in his diary: 'Hitler is enraged.'[28]

The second meeting was, apparently, a little calmer. Goebbels was no longer present – the *Gauleiter* for the Berlin section had gone to his office in the party building in the Voßstraße in order to co-ordinate the party's actions during the night. Present instead were Vice Chancellor von Papen, who, as Reich commissioner for Prussia, was formally Göring's superior, and Undersecretary Ludwig Grauert. During the meeting, the men discussed the consequences of the alleged communist arson attack for Prussia. In the first instance, the series of arrests requested in the Reichstag meeting was confirmed. This was officially underpinned by the first emergency decree passed by the Hitler government on 4 February 1933 – 'For the Protection of the German People' – which was predominantly aimed at limiting competition from all parties critical of the NSDAP. On the same legal basis, the government issued a ban on all KPD newspapers until further notice, and on all social democratic publications for the next two weeks. It was also agreed that an extraordinary ministerial meeting should take place the following morning. Finally, Grauert suggested passing a further emergency decree to deal with 'arson and acts of terrorism'. This was similar to another emergency decree that had been agreed on and submitted to the Reich president for signature only a few hours earlier: the 'Decree against Treason and Treasonous Activities', often confused with the 'Decree for the Protection of People and State'. Grauert did not want to extend either of these decrees; he wanted to issue an

Officers collecting evidence on 28 February or 1 March were faced with a scene of destruction at the burned-out plenary chamber. (Private collection)

additional one. Minister of the Interior Frick was tasked with drafting this new decree.[29]

Meanwhile, based on the (legally questionable) emergency decree 'For the Protection of the German People', passed three weeks earlier, the first police actions were underway. According to article 22, it was now possible to arrest someone 'in the interest of public safety' if there was strong reason to suspect that they had betrayed state secrets or intended to commit treason. In addition, the police could now arrest anyone suspected of a crime involving a firearm for up to three months. This ambiguous clause facilitated a merciless attack on communism in Germany, which was fully exploited by the authorities. The official register of communist MPs, which had been held by the IA division of the Berlin police force for years, had already partly been updated in the second half of 1932 during the Papen government. Now this was quickly turned into a hit list – with current addresses, if available – and arrest warrants were issued. At around 3.25 a.m., all German border control officials were instructed that no KPD MPs were to leave the country; Berlin Tempelhof airport had already received the same order ten minutes earlier.

That first night, around 250 police detectives and policemen were on duty. In Berlin alone, around 130 communist MPs and well-known leftists were arrested within twelve hours of Göring's order; seventy more in the night leading into 1 March. Among them were several KPD Reichstag members and members of the *Landtag* [state parliament], thus breaching their immunity, although truly prominent politicians such as Ernst Thälmann, Walter Ulbricht or Willi Münzenberg were spared. However, communist journalists such as Ernst Schneller, intellectuals such as Werner Scholem and well-known Hitler opponents such as Carl von Ossietzki, Erich Mühsam and the lawyer Hans Litten were arrested. Police action was not limited to Berlin: in the district of Hanover, 140 genuine or alleged communists were arrested by the

Opposite top: Part of the plenary chamber's panelling had crashed to the ground during the fire, making the firefighting operations very dangerous. (National Archives, Washington DC)

Opposite bottom: Rubble in the burned-out plenary chamber. The name plate belonged to the NSDAP MP Ludwig Münchmeyer, a former pastor and nasty rabble-rouser. (National Archives, Washington DC)

evening of 28 February; in Cologne it was eighty. Those arrested were generally taken to ordinary prisons and were, on the whole, treated decently – so far, the auxiliary police, made up of the SA and SS, had hardly been employed.[30]

After the late meeting at the Prussian interior ministry, Hitler had rushed to the editorial offices of the *Völkischer Beobachter* in Berlin's newspaper district in order to edit the next day's edition. And indeed, the following morning, on 28 February, the headlines of the NSDAP's main paper were sharply critical of the KPD; it appears that Hitler's choleric outburst had been more or less directly reproduced in print. After this, the chancellor returned to the Hotel Kaiserhof, joined by Goebbels, who had just written an aggressive editorial for the next edition of the Nazi evening paper *Der Angriff*. The new state of affairs was also reflected in the fact that Rudolf Diels, the head of the Prussian political police, reported back to party official Goebbels – something that would have been unthinkable just a few weeks earlier. At 5.30 a.m., Hitler, Göring and Goebbels took a break from their non-stop activities. A meeting for the ministers to discuss the next steps had been arranged at the Reich chancellery only a few hours later, at 11.00 a.m.

It is likely that staff at the interior ministry worked through the night – head of department Wilhelm Frick had requested the draft of a new emergency decree by the time the Cabinet was due to meet. Known as the 'Reichstag Fire Decree', the 'Decree of the Reich President for the Protection of the People and State' was published on 28 February. For a long time it was regarded as the 'Basic Law of the Third Reich' – after all, the decree suspended the most important civil rights of the Weimar constitution, including the rights of personal freedom, the freedom of the press, the freedom of speech, the freedom to organise and assemble, and the privacy of postal communications. In addition, articles 4 and 5 established draconian penalties for certain offences, such as high treason, arson and other 'political' crimes. The decree remained in effect until 1945. However, the fundamental clauses of the 'Reichstag Fire Decree', especially the abrogation of basic rights, had been copied almost verbatim from the template for emergency decrees in 1919. During the time of the Weimar Republic, precisely these clauses had been enforced again and again: several times between 1919 and 1921, in 1923 and again in 1932. Even the clause in article 2, which allowed the declaration of a civil state of emergency, was not entirely new – it had already existed in 1920/21. However, that had been the exception; in most cases, the *Reichswehr* had assumed executive authority during the political crises of the first German democracy.

But this is exactly what Hitler wanted to avoid. From 30 January 1933 onwards, he had counted on the fact that the Reichstag would transfer legislative power to the government – and thus to him as chancellor – by majority vote, and therefore disempower itself. This would make unnecessary any further emergency decrees that could only be issued by the Reich president. However, this would only work if the military did not become involved in domestic politics and if the NSDAP claimed a significant victory in the upcoming elections. Perhaps Hitler really was concerned that the arson attack jeopardised his plan – certainly it would mean a bitter setback for his strategy should Hindenburg once again employ the *Reichswehr* in these exceptional circumstances.

Reichsgesetzblatt

Teil I

| 1933 | Ausgegeben zu Berlin, den 28. Februar 1933 | Nr. 17 |

Inhalt: Verordnung des Reichspräsidenten zum Schutz von Volk und Staat. Vom 28. Februar 1933 ...... S. 83

Verordnung des Reichspräsidenten zum Schutz von Volk und Staat. Vom 28. Februar 1933.

Auf Grund des Artikels 48 Abs. 2 der Reichsverfassung wird zur Abwehr kommunistischer staatsgefährdender Gewaltakte folgendes verordnet:

§ 1

Die Artikel 114, 115, 117, 118, 123, 124 und 153 der Verfassung des Deutschen Reichs werden bis auf weiteres außer Kraft gesetzt. Es sind daher Beschränkungen der persönlichen Freiheit, des Rechts der freien Meinungsäußerung, einschließlich der Pressefreiheit, des Vereins- und Versammlungsrechts, Eingriffe in das Brief-, Post-, Telegraphen- und Fernsprechgeheimnis, Anordnungen von Haussuchungen und von Beschlagnahmen sowie Beschränkungen des Eigentums auch außerhalb der sonst hierfür bestimmten gesetzlichen Grenzen zulässig.

§ 2

Werden in einem Lande die zur Wiederherstellung der öffentlichen Sicherheit und Ordnung nötigen Maßnahmen nicht getroffen, so kann die Reichsregierung insoweit die Befugnisse der obersten Landesbehörde vorübergehend wahrnehmen.

§ 3

Die Behörden der Länder und Gemeinden (Gemeindeverbände) haben auf Grund des § 2 erlassenen Anordnungen der Reichsregierung im Rahmen ihrer Zuständigkeit Folge zu leisten.

§ 4

Wer den von den obersten Landesbehörden oder den ihnen nachgeordneten Behörden zur Durchführung dieser Verordnung erlassenen Anordnungen oder den von der Reichsregierung gemäß § 2 erlassenen Anordnungen zuwiderhandelt oder wer zu solcher Zuwiderhandlung auffordert oder anreizt, wird, soweit nicht die Tat nach anderen Vorschriften mit einer schwereren Strafe bedroht ist, mit Gefängnis nicht unter einem Monat oder mit Geldstrafe von 150 bis zu 15 000 Reichsmark bestraft.

Wer durch Zuwiderhandlung nach Abs. 1 eine gemeine Gefahr für Menschenleben herbeiführt, wird mit Zuchthaus, bei mildernden Umständen mit Gefängnis nicht unter sechs Monaten und, wenn die Zuwiderhandlung den Tod eines Menschen verursacht, mit dem Tode, bei mildernden Umständen mit Zuchthaus nicht unter zwei Jahren bestraft. Daneben kann auf Vermögenseinziehung erkannt werden.

Wer zu einer gemeingefährlichen Zuwiderhandlung (Abs. 2) auffordert oder anreizt, wird mit Zuchthaus, bei mildernden Umständen mit Gefängnis nicht unter drei Monaten bestraft.

§ 5

Mit dem Tode sind die Verbrechen zu bestrafen, die das Strafgesetzbuch in den §§ 81 (Hochverrat), 229 (Giftbeibringung), 307 (Brandstiftung), 311 (Explosion), 312 (Überschwemmung), 315 Abs. 2 (Beschädigung von Eisenbahnanlagen), 324 (gemeingefährliche Vergiftung) mit lebenslangem Zuchthaus bedroht.

Mit dem Tode oder, soweit nicht bisher eine schwerere Strafe angedroht ist, mit lebenslangem Zuchthaus oder mit Zuchthaus bis zu 15 Jahren wird bestraft:

1. Wer es unternimmt, den Reichspräsidenten oder ein Mitglied oder einen Kommissar der Reichsregierung oder einer Landesregierung zu töten oder wer zu einer solchen Tötung auffordert, sich erbietet, ein solches Erbieten annimmt oder eine solche Tötung mit einem anderen verabredet;
2. wer in den Fällen des § 115 Abs. 2 des Strafgesetzbuchs (schwerer Aufruhr) oder des § 125 Abs. 2 des Strafgesetzbuchs (schwerer Landfriedensbruch) die Tat mit Waffen oder in bewußtem und gewolltem Zusammenwirken mit einem Bewaffneten begeht;
3. wer eine Freiheitsberaubung (§ 239) des Strafgesetzbuchs in der Absicht begeht, sich des der Freiheit Beraubten als Geisel im politischen Kampfe zu bedienen.

§ 6

Diese Verordnung tritt mit dem Tage der Verkündung in Kraft.

Berlin, den 28. Februar 1933.

Der Reichspräsident
von Hindenburg

Der Reichskanzler
Adolf Hitler

Der Reichsminister des Innern
Frick

Der Reichsminister der Justiz
Dr. Gürtner

Just one day after the fire, on the evening of 28 February 1933, the 'Decree for the Protection of the People and the State', later known as the 'Reichstag Fire Decree', was published. As a result, a civil state of emergency was declared over the entire Reich. (Kellerhoff archive)

The NSDAP's nationalist-conservative coalition partners were aware that the clause referring to a nationwide civil state of emergency was the critical one; until now, this extreme measure had been restricted to certain regions. According to the minutes, it was only this clause that was debated when Reich Minister of the Interior Frick presented his proposal to the Cabinet. As a result of the discussion, two minor amendments were made.[31]

By exaggerating the gravity of the situation, Hitler was able to persuade the rest of the predominantly non-National Socialist Cabinet. According to the minutes, 'the chancellor explained that the situation urgently called for an uncompromising stance towards the KPD'. He added that, from a psychological point of view, it was the right moment for a confrontation and that it was therefore pointless to wait any longer. Hitler added that 'the KPD was willing to use extreme measures and that the fight against them should not be impeded by legal considerations'. The chancellor was, then, openly announcing a breach of law. Yet no opposition was voiced. On the contrary: the nationalist minister of justice even suggested including further draconian measures in the act, especially for the use of 'poison as a means of terrorism'. Göring remarked that 'a single perpetrator would have been unable to orchestrate this arson attack'. Although he accurately summarised van der Lubbe's statement, he questioned its credibility: 'The detainee claims to have carried out the act alone, but this is highly unlikely. He, Reichstag Minister Göring, suspected the involvement of six or seven perpetrators.' He made one more important announcement: 'Today, 2,000 SA and SS men will be marching through the city to support the police.'[32]

The acting commissar for the Prussian ministry of the interior gave the men an unequivocal message: 'I have been told that the communists are planning to shut down the electric mains, transport and all other providers of vital services through acts of violence or sabotage in the very near future. Explosives for these acts of sabotage are said to be in good supply.' He added that members of the communist *Rotfrontkämpferbund* had been advised 'to make use of their firearm immediately and in every case should they encounter national units'. Göring had told the Berlin SA chief the same. With this, he turned the paramilitary groups loose: the order effectively gave them carte blanche to fight political opponents by all available means. The result was an unprecedented explosion of violence.

The Cabinet met again on the afternoon of 28 February. In the meantime, Hitler and Vice Chancellor Papen had been to see Hindenburg. Hitler told him that during the last few years, 15 tons of explosives had been stolen in Germany and were now in the hands of the KPD. The chancellor offered no proof for this, and the head of state did not ask for any. By now, the few changes demanded by the coalition partners had been incorporated into the new decree. The chancellery began to leak internal information to the *Berliner Tageblatt*: 'We have learned that there is no intention of imposing a state of emergency. However, the measures taken against the communist threat will have the same effect as a state of emergency.' During the second ministerial meeting that day, which began at 4.15 p.m., the Cabinet members briefly discussed article 2. Another minor change was made, after which Frick's draft was accepted and passed onto the Reich president to sign. The new emergency decree was announced that same evening, and by 7.45 p.m. Frick was already discussing it with the state representatives. The 'Decree against Treason Toward the German People', which had already been agreed one day before the 'Reichstag Fire Decree', even appeared after the 'Decree For the Protection of the German People' in the *Reichsgesetzblatt* [Reich Law Gazette].[33]

In the evening of February 28, large numbers of SA and SS men were called into action in Berlin. In some cases they supported the regular police, but for the most part they arbitrarily arrested political opponents on the initiative of their local superiors. These gangs of thugs no longer consulted lists, and certainly did not follow the provisions of the criminal law. They also did not take 'their' prisoners to official prisons, but to secret locations, often to the cellars underneath their *Sturmlokal* [SA meeting place], empty buildings or old barracks. There, from the early days of March, the prisoners were brutally beaten and mistreated; this is where SA men 'settled scores'. Soon, there were dozens of such illegal prisons, not only in hidden-away places, but also in the city centre. In the cellar of Friedrichstraße 234, an SA *Sturmlokal*, up to 300 political opponents are said to have been tortured at the same time. Men were beaten up in the equipment rooms of the water tower in Prenzlauer Berg, in the back room of a pub in Goethestraße 14 in Charlottenburg, in the SA *Sturmlokal* in Liebenwalder Straße in Wedding, as well as in the skittle club in Petersburger Straße in Friedrichshain. It is not known how many such torture cellars existed in those first weeks of March; overall it is estimated that there were more than 150 'wild concentration camps' in Berlin between March 1933 and June 1934. Some of these were used for only a few nights, whereas others were used for months. In the two weeks after the Reichstag fire alone, 7,784 people were officially taken into 'protective custody' in Prussia. Yet this figure only includes twenty-four of the thirty-four Prussian administrative districts, which means that the more accurate figure up to 15 March is likely to be closer to 10,000, or more. There were riots in other states too, for instance in Thuringia. In Bavaria, where Minister-President Heinrich Held, a Catholic and conservative man, still retained firm control, the situation remained quiet for the moment.[34]

The SA in Berlin was ruthless – so brutal, that even Göring felt compelled to intervene. Thus, the police prevented a planned shooting of prisoners on 3 March in the SA *Sturmlokal* Drechsel in Spandau. The men were released, though many were soon arrested and mistreated again. Göring's circular about the 'Reichstag Fire Decree' on the same day also seems to have been issued to prevent an escalation of events:

> The permitted additional measures laid out in the decree are to be used primarily to deal with communists, as well as those who work with communists and who pursue their illegal goals, even if only indirectly. To avoid mistakes, I would like to point out that if actions against relatives or institutions that are not part of communist, anarchist or social-democratic parties or organisations become necessary, these will only be covered by the 'Decree for the Protection of the German People' if they serve the purpose of fighting communist efforts in the broadest sense.

SA boss Ernst Röhm reminded his men of 'loyalty and discipline', and that 'those who cause displeasure among their ranks, agitate or retaliate on their own initiative will be firmly dealt with'. At the same time, however, Röhm promised: 'Soon the day of retribution and atonement for all your hardship and persecution will come.' However, the brown-shirted thugs were not interested in Göring's subtle distinctions and Röhm's promises – they wanted to 'enjoy' their new-found power immediately. For instance, on 6 March a group of SA troopers from Charlottenburg kidnapped the American Nathaniel Wolff and took him to a flat in a summer house in the well-to-do Knesebackstraße. There he was forced, in writing, to 'confess' that he was Jewish and that he would leave Germany the same day and never return. Wolff also 'confirmed' with his signature that he had not been mistreated or stolen from.[35]

During the morning's Cabinet meeting on 28 February 1933, Hitler had announced that now, after the Reichstag fire, 'he did not doubt that the Reich government would win 51 per cent in the election'. In reality, the NSDAP chief was hoping for even more: he wanted a parliamentary majority for his own party in order to get rid of their inconvenient, if compliant, coalition partner, the *Deutschnationale Volkspartei*. However, despite the brutal obstruction of opposition parties and the biased support of public-service broadcasting, the Reichstag election on 5 March 1933 did not deliver the desired result. Nationally, the NSDAP only received 43.9 per cent of the votes, which meant that it was still dependent on its reactionary coalition partner, who received 8 per cent of the votes. Despite this result, Hitler called for a 'National Socialist revolution'; he had already called for a 'national rising' after his appointment as chancellor. Backed by the emergency decrees passed in February 1933, the few remaining non-National Socialist state governments were disempowered and replaced with Reich commissars. The NSDAP's often brutal seizure of power continued in local authorities, too. In Cologne, for instance, the mayor, Konrad Adenauer, was driven out of the town hall. The persecution of communists now took place on a national level – by the end of April 1933, at least 40,000 political opponents had been arrested and, often, mistreated.

In the capital, Hitler was working hard to expand his position of power. He and Hindenburg had been in agreement about the planned pseudo-legal coup since early February. The use of an enabling law, which transferred legislative powers from parliament to the Reich government, was not new in the context of the Weimar constitution. To the contrary, several such laws had existed between 1919 and 1924 – Hitler could build on this. However, as the election had not yielded the clear victory Hitler had hoped for, he had to continue his tactical manoeuvring. First of all, Göring perfidiously arranged the retraction of the KPD's seats: the NSDAP and DNVP enforced, by means of a formal request, the rule that any member of parliament could be barred if they had unauthorised absences. In addition, all communist ministers that were present were arrested, despite their immunity; the rest had fled abroad

Real and alleged political opponents were forcefully taken to a large number of basements or rear buildings during the early days of March. Often, the victims – mainly communists, other leftists and Jews – were brutally mistreated. (National Archives, Washington DC)

or had gone into hiding. Moreover, the NSDAP put pressure on the catholic *Zentrum* [Centre Party], while the liberal parties, already reduced to splinter groups, also buckled. Thus the prerequisites for a two-thirds majority for the 'Law to Remedy the Distress of People and Reich' – better known as the Enabling Act – were set, voted for on 23 March in the hastily converted Kroll opera house opposite the Reichstag building. This created the basis for a 'Führer State'. Only the SPD voted against it.[36]

On the Enabling Act's first day of validity, the government passed Hitler's new law regarding the imposition and implementation of the death penalty. The sole purpose of this was to increase the impending punishment for Marinus van der Lubbe. The law stated that the threat of punishment under article 5 of the 'Reichstag Fire Decree' 'also applies to those crimes that were committed between 31 January and 28 February'. It was, therefore, also valid retrospectively, which constitutes a violation of one of the most fundamental legal principles, the '*nulla poena sine lege*' principle ('no penalty without a law'). On 2 March 1933, the chancellor had announced to the Cabinet that it would have been better 'to hang the culprit straight away'. Wilhelm Frick also thought it was 'imperative to hang van der Lubbe straight away – on the Königsplatz', thus in front of the Reichstag. He referred to a report by three respected criminal law experts that he had commissioned: 'Even though the current law only stipulates penal servitude, it should be possible to retrospectively change the verdict for such a despicable crime to death by hanging. The "nulla poena sine lege" principle should not be applied unconditionally in this case.' Franz Schlegelberger, the state secretary in the Reich ministry of justice, appealed once more and commissioned a counter-opinion, but then acquiesced and approved the tightening of the existing death penalty law himself. The Dutch envoy aptly interpreted this new law as 'apparently intended directly for van der Lubbe'. The foreign minister Konstantin von Neurath, a diplomat with the *Deutschnationale Volkspartei*, was merciless. In his view, the new law 'did most certainly not violate international law' and he assured that the trial would be dealt with 'lawfully in every way'. The opposite was the case: by way of the new law, Marinus van der Lubbe had already been sentenced to death months before his trial.[37]

UNDER SUSPICION

DOUBTS ABOUT THE NAZIS' VERSION AND THE CAMPAIGN FROM THE PARISIAN EXILE

I t is not known who first speculated that it could have been the National Socialists themselves who set fire to the Reichstag. If we can assume Sefton Delmer's recollection to be correct, the earliest known, albeit indirect, suspicion came from NSDAP ideologue Alfred Rosenberg. It would have been around 10.00 p.m. on 27 February 1933 – the fire brigade was still trying to prevent the fire from spreading beyond the plenary chamber, and Hitler and Goebbels had not yet arrived – when Rosenberg said to the British journalist: 'I hope this wasn't done by our boys. It's exactly the kind of stupid thing they might do.' Among the crowd, too, the assumption spread that it was more likely to have been Hitler supporters than his opponents. It was obvious to any careful observer that in this political climate the fire would be beneficial to the government; just six days before the election, it would serve as a welcome excuse to further increase the pressure on political opponents. And as rumours are apparently confirmed most effectively by the ostensibly innocent question 'cui bono?' – 'to whose benefit?' – many eyewitnesses assumed, already during the fire-fighting operations, that only the Nazis themselves were the likely culprits.[38]

The conviction that it must have been several people who started the fire also began to spread through the crowds. This rumour was likely started by the firefighters and police officers who spoke to journalists and onlookers during their short breaks – to them it was obvious that it had been a whole group of arsonists. Chief Constable Buwert, for instance, said it looked as though 'people were running around in there with torches'. Police Lieutenant Lateit told his men to draw their weapons to 'prevent the culprits' potential escape' from the building. Helmut Poeschel, who had caught van der Lubbe red-handed, said during his first interview: 'Looking at the fire, I did wonder whether there were more people involved.' Other eye-witnesses made similar statements, such as Fire Chief Gempp, who told journalists about a 'trail' on the carpets on the main floor, caused by a liquid fire accelerant, on the night of the fire. Based on such speculations, the *Morgenpost* reported that 'piles of cleaning rags soaked in petrol' had been found. The paper suggested: 'There are many possibilities as to who may be responsible for this crime.' However, the Berlin press did not go any further. After only a month of a NSDAP-led government, journalists were too concerned about their paper being banned to speculate more freely. The newspapers of 28 February thus only reported the official version, which incriminated the communists, as well as a few careful hints that it could also have been a single arsonist.[39]

A very different view was taken among those critical of National Socialism. Erich Ebermayer, a lawyer and writer from Leipzig, and the son of the former chief public prosecutor of the Weimar Republic, remembers: 'The midnight news had just started on the radio when I heard the news reader's agitated voice: "The Reichstag is on fire!" Every conversation in the small café stopped. We then heard that communists had set the German Reichstag in Berlin on fire that evening.' Ebermayer and his friends, none of them Hitler supporters, could not believe what they had just heard:

> We were shocked. Such an act of madness, just before the elections, just before the day that had been so carefully planned and termed the 'Day of National Awakening' by Goebbels – we couldn't believe it. What could have driven the communists to such a herostratic act of desperation? Didn't they realise that this played into the Nazis' hands?

Ebermayer went home straight away: 'My father was still sitting at his desk, working. I told him the news. He was silent for a few seconds, and then said, in his strong Bavarian accent: "They obviously did that themselves!"'

Wolfgang Stresemann, the late foreign secretary's son, also blamed the Nazis when he heard about the arson attack the following morning: 'My phone started ringing at 7 a.m. It was my uncle […]: "Just imagine, the Nazis set fire to the Reichstag, the whole building is aflame." My answer: "What, is their election campaign going so badly?"' Harry Graf Kessler, a bohemian, noted: 'Nobody I have spoken to believes the story of the "communist arsonists". Besides, the NSDAP people must be pleased about the destruction of the hateful Reichstag, irrespective of any political purpose it may have.' In his report to Paris, the French ambassador François-Poncet chose his words carefully: 'Several details are confusing in the matter of the Reichstag fire.' He too assumed that large amounts of combustible material had been secured in the parliament building, but was hesitant to commit to any one version of events:

The possibility of the arrested Dutchman being the culprit, and the fire having been caused in the way he describes, cannot be ruled out completely. However, it is also possible that not all aspects of this version of events correspond to the truth, and that the police and the government would have exploited the arson attack in the same way had every detail of the incident been staged.[40]

Many foreign journalists were less reticent than their German colleagues. Already on 1 March 1933, several international newspapers published articles that, depending on their political leaning, contained either speculations or accusations that Hitler's government, and especially Göring, was responsible for the fire. The Parisian daily newspaper *Le Temps* reported on 1 March:

The official communiqué is clearly designed to outrage the population and turn it against the left-wing opposition. There is no way to verify the claims made by the police. One can merely note that the Reichstag fire came at an opportune moment for propaganda purposes in the upcoming election campaign.

On 3 March, the *Daily Telegraph* reported: 'No sensible German believes the theory that communists set the Reichstag on fire.' The Soviet newspapers *Iswestia* and *Prawda* accused 'German capitalists' of the arson attack and referred to it as a 'provocation', while the *Chicago Daily Tribune* speculated that the Nazis were involved. Hermann Göring was furious about such reports, as he made clear during a ministerial meeting on 2 March 1933 when he said that 'it ought to be checked whether something can be done about the foreign press, as some reports suggested that he himself [Göring] had set the Reichstag on fire'.[41]

The serious accusations put forward by Hitler's government and the illegal arrests of hundreds of communists served to intensify the debate in the press between the political left and right in the press at the beginning of March. Over the past years, both sides had, again and again, invented defamatory stories in the often bloody battle for power. This practice now continued: National Socialist newspapers reported, for instance, that Ernst Torgler, chairman of the KPD parliamentary group in the Reichstag, had been arrested for his involvement in the arson attack just two days after the fire. In reality, he had presented himself to the police on 28 February 1933 and vehemently denied any involvement:

> In response to some reports in the press, which I was made aware of this morning, I would like to clarify the following regarding the Reichstag fire: […] The entire party, as well as I personally, condemn such acts of terror, or rather capital offences. In addition, such an act would make absolutely no political sense just before the elections; on the contrary, it would be madness.

Despite his immunity and the fact that Torgler had appeared of his own free will, he was taken into police custody.

The KPD reacted quickly to the accusations voiced by Göring and Hitler. A leaflet by their faction in the *Sächsischer Landtag* [Saxon state parliament] appeared on 28 February in Dresden: 'Hired arsonists set Reichstag building aflame! Act of violence by fascist reactionary force!' The production of this leaflet had been possible because the series of arrests in Saxony began later than elsewhere. In Berlin, where the party had already gone underground, the Central Committee of the Communist Party of Germany issued a statement on 1 March in which it condemned the 'Reichstag fire provocation staged by the Nazis' and demanded the suspension of all the coercive measures put in place by Hitler's government. On the same day, the KPD issued its first statement abroad, in the Swiss communist newspaper

Rundschau über Politik, Wirtschaft und Arbeiterbewegung: 'The arson attack on the Reichstag building is nothing but a large-scale provocation aimed at the communist party and the struggling working class.' The press in Moscow was of the same opinion: 'The fascists will do anything to follow through with their pogrom, even if it means burning the Reichstag to the ground.' These articles, written less than twenty-four hours after the arson attack, were based on nothing but rumours and one press release.[42]

The NSDAP responded with even more outrageous accusations. In the days preceding the election, Hitler held speeches in Breslau, Berlin, Hamburg and Königsberg, where he repeatedly argued that the 'elimination of Marxism' was 'crucial to the vital interests of German workers'. Göring also held public speeches, and apparently received a positive response. Goebbels, piqued, later said about his rival's speech: 'I'm listening to the end. Too much "I". "I, Hitler and the German people will crush the KPD."' The NSDAP newspaper *Völkischer Beobachter* made up a story about 'secret plans for a revolt', but could not offer any evidence for this. The investigators at police headquarters were also unable to find any concrete evidence to support the theory of a conspiracy. For this reason, they decided to use an unusual approach: they published a photo of van der Lubbe and offered a reward of 20,000 *Reichsmark* for 'any information that can help to identify the accomplices, instigators and those involved behind the scenes'. The result was predictable: in no time, the newly established task force, led by Rudolf Braschwitz, was flooded with allegations and supposedly important observations – including, for instance, a sighting of van der Lubbe in the Saxon village of Sörnewitz, and information about a teenager from Berlin called Heinz Walter Weinberg, who was said to be connected to the arson attack. Checking all these 'leads' was time-consuming, and brought no new insights. There was one exception, however: a waiter reported three men, assumed to be Russians, who had apparently met van der Lubbe in a restaurant in the Postdamer Straße. On 9 March, he informed the police that the three men had returned to the restaurant. The criminal police seized the opportunity and arrested three Bulgarian communists: Wassili Taneff, Blagoi Popoff and Georgi Dimitroff, the head of the Western European Office of Comintern [Communist International]. Even though their link to van der Lubbe was tenuous, they were accused – like Torgler – of being the 'masterminds' behind the arson attack.[43]

The arrest of the three Bulgarians and the brutal persecution of German communists put pressure on the now-underground KPD propagandists. In order to publish 'news', even though there was none, they circulated fake stories, for instance: 'On the recommendation of the *Horst-Wessel-Sturm*, the fascist Göring had the Reichstag set aflame to mark the beginning of the pogrom against the communist party and the revolutionary proletariat.' There was, however, no link whatsoever between the fifth Berlin SA *Sturm* and the arson attack, and it was hardly ever mentioned again in subsequent communist publications. That particular SA division, named after the SA leader Horst Wessel who was assassinated in 1930, was likely singled out because it was based in Friedrichshain, a primarily communist district. It was in this KPD heartland that the NSDAP had been so successfully canvassing supporters, many of them former KPD-voters. Yet despite the violent pressure from the police, SA and SS, the KPD did surprisingly well in the Reichstag election on 5 March. Even though the Nazis had regularly disrupted their campaign rallies, and their newspapers had been banned – first on and off since the beginning of February, and then entirely from 28 February – and even though their MPs had been persecuted and often tortured, the party lost just under a fifth of votes in greater Berlin, compared to their highest election result in November 1932.[44]

In the meantime, Willi Münzenberg, formerly Germany's 'red press baron', had fled to Paris. From his exile he organised a large-scale propaganda campaign against the Nazis. With popular and successful titles such as the *Arbeiter-Illustrierten Zeitung* and the *Welt am Abend*, Münzenberg had been the main opponent of reactionary publisher Alfred Hugenberg in the past. With the help of a small team, Münzenberg collated information about the brutal persecution of communists in Germany and distributed dossiers about the crimes committed by the Hitler-Hugenberg government to newspapers throughout Europe (by no means only communist papers). They 'supplemented' their collections with fake evidence to support the theory, now widespread around the world, that the Nazis were also responsible for the Reichstag fire. Thus, supposedly genuine documents that denounced Marinus van der Lubbe as 'effeminate' and as 'in every fibre of his being homosexual', as well as apparently having been on SA boss Röhm's 'love list', appear to have been created in Münzenberg's office in Paris. In addition, the young Dutchman was said to be a 'pathological liar'.[45]

The most well-known fabrication was circulated during the second week of April 1933. This 'memorandum about the Reichstag arson attack' contained a description of how the Nazis had set fire to the building:

> Meanwhile the men who had been appointed by Göring entered the Reichstag through the heating ducts leading to it from the president of the Reichstag's Palais under the command of the Silesian SA leader and MP Heines. Each of the selected SA and SS men had been assigned an exact spot where to start the fire. When the lookout in the Reichstag reported that the communist MPs Torgler and Koenen had left the building, the SA special unit got down to work. With so much manpower, the fire quickly took hold. Then they all returned to the Palais, where they

changed back into their SA uniforms and from where they could easily slip away. The only person left was van der Lubbe, who, as a precaution, had put a Dutch passport, a communist flyer about the united front, a few photographs of himself and, allegedly, even a membership card of a Dutch communist splinter group into his back trouser pocket. Lo and behold – there was the desired fire.

Göring's Prussian interior ministry became aware of this 'memorandum' on 18 April at the very latest – it was on this day that a copy was filed. However, it only became clear how politically explosive it was eight days later, when the *Manchester Guardian* published the memorandum in two parts on 26 and 27 April. According to the newspaper's leader, the exposé's source had close links to the German Nationals in Hitler's Cabinet. The DNVP ministers thus appeared to be blocking Hitler, and to be putting up resistance to the NSDAP's absolute rule. The 'memorandum' was an internationally successful coup. The *New York Times* reported that it had triggered a 'diplomatic storm'. Predictably, the NSDAP was incensed; the *Völkischer Beobachter* published a furious response to the article in the *Manchester Guardian*: 'A supposed special correspondent of said newspaper publishes an article about the Reichstag fire. Titled "Germany in April", it deals with the event in a totally inflammatory and mendacious way – including the outrageous accusation that the "arsonists are members of this government's own Cabinet."' The *Telegraphen-Union*, a pro-government newspaper, reacted similarly. An 'accusation like this', it said, was 'unparalleled in the history of civilised nations'. The Reich government is said to have advised staff at its embassy in London to 'condemn such publications in the harshest of terms'. However, this did not diminish the article's success in any way. In fact, the text now also appeared in a newspaper in Basel. This version was copied onto templates and circulated in Germany – the special commission's records on the Reichstag fire include more than half a dozen copies of the five-page pamphlet.[46]

At the beginning of May 1933, it became known that Ernst Oberfohren, who had led the DNVP faction in the Reichstag until the end of March, had shot himself. It did not take long for him to be named as the author of the 'memorandum' – it was speculated that he had either committed suicide or been killed by Goebbels' or Göring's men after its publication. Even the *Manchester Guardian* reported that the text had been written 'at the request of Dr Oberfohren'. The article stated: 'Dr Oberfohren's link to the exposé had to remain a secret while he was still alive, but there is no longer any need for secrecy after his death.' Soon, the 'memorandum' was published as a booklet. Unlike the English edition, the German edition included a photograph of Oberfohren, and explicitly named him as the author. At first glance, it appeared to incriminate the Nazis: an exposé from a politician who, although perhaps reactionary, had always been opposed to Hitler and who, after his party leader had joined forces with the NSDAP, had felt remorse about the arson attack, resigned, and then put his insider knowledge on paper. It was commonly assumed that, after publishing the text anonymously, the Nazis had found him out and had either driven him to committing suicide or had simply shot him themselves.[47]

However, neither Oberfohren nor any other top politician from the DNVP could have been the author of the text, or even have commissioned it. It stated:

> Already in one of the first Cabinet meetings the National Socialist minority had tried, unsuccessfully, to push through a ban on the communist party. Mr Hugenberg had argued that the public may become alarmed by uncontrolled or uncontrollable shootings, or other acts of violence by communists or workers of the radical left which could occur once the party's legality was no longer a consideration.

In reality, however, the exact opposite was the case: DNVP leader Alfred Hugenberg had pushed for a ban on the KPD, while Hitler had argued against it – this is evident from the undisputedly genuine Cabinet minutes, which in 1933 had of course been top secret. During the first meeting of Hitler's government on 30 January, the trade and industry secretary of the DNVP had demanded the adoption of tough measures against the communists. Hugenberg's statement was recorded in the minutes as follows: 'He stated that in his view it was impossible to avoid the suppression of the KPD […]. He added that he was doubtful that the suppression of the KPD would lead to a general strike and that he would choose the KPD's suppression over a re-election.' Hitler, on the other hand, feared that 'a potential ban on the KPD may lead to serious domestic conflict and, eventually, a general strike'. In his view, a re-election was much less risky than a ban on communists. This reversal of the true course of events alone proves that the author of the 'memorandum' was unfamiliar with the goings-on in the Cabinet – which renders the text practically worthless as evidence about the Reichstag fire. If the author had no access to internal affairs, then he was also unable to offer any 'true' information about the arson attack. The articles about the alleged murder of Oberfohren, or his forced suicide, were also wrong – the former minister had committed suicide because he had been defeated by Hugenberg in the battle for power within the DNVP and 'in his despair had chosen suicide', his widow confided twenty years later.[48]

Other details in the 'memorandum' also turned out to be incorrect. For instance, the man said to be the arsonist team's ringleader, SA leader Edmund Heines, had in fact been in Gleiwitz on the evening of 27 February 1933 – 450km from Berlin. It was also suggested in the text that the British correspondent Sefton Delmer had sat down with Hitler, Goebbels and Göring before knowledge about the fire had reached the public: 'Thus the cosy foursome waited for their fire.'

In reality, Delmer had been in his flat. While it is true that he later accompanied Hitler into the burning Reichstag, he did not know the NSDAP leader nearly well enough to have been invited to Goebbels' flat. In this case, the forgers had not read the article in the *Daily Express* carefully enough – one particular phrase gave a clear indication of the 'memorandum's' true origin:

> Goebbels and those closest to him paid particular attention to the looming developments in the labour force. They clearly felt that a united front of workers, combining social democrats and communists, would become a reality, in spite of their rejection of the social-democratic leaders and the communist leadership's ineptitude.

This phrase, commonly found in the KPD's anti-social-democratic propaganda, had accidently been included in this text – a text that had supposedly been written by a DNVP politician. The same applied to the claim that DNVP ministers had organised a putsch for the night following the Reichstag election. According to the memorandum, Reich President Hindenburg had planned to use the arson attack by the National Socialists to unseat Hitler and establish a 'national government' with the help of the *Reichswehr* and the DNVP. Similar scenarios had already been published in communist pamphlets in 1932. However, in reality Hindenburg was apprehensive about deploying the *Reichswehr* in this way; indeed, this reluctance had been the main reason why he had given in to Franz von Papen and had agreed to appoint Hitler as Reich chancellor at the end of January 1933.

Despite these flaws, the 'Oberfohren-memorandum' formed the basis for Willi Münzenberg's next attack on the Hitler government. He collated the various fabrications in a book entitled *Braunbuch* [*Brown Book*], which was published in several languages and was widely circulated. Descriptions of the assaults on communists by

National Socialists in the spring of 1933 – claims that were largely true – formed the most politically explosive parts of the 383-page German edition. However, all references to the Reichstag fire were based on false information. The *Braunbuch* was intended as a prelude to the most important attack on Hitler by the exiled KPD: the 'counter trial' that was supposed to 'prove' that the Nazis were responsible for the Reichstag fire.[49]

6

THE TRIALS

THE TRIAL IN LEIPZIG AND THE 'COUNTER TRIAL' IN LONDON

'As you know, we were given the task of finding an international court of law that could act as a sort of counter-court of law,' Willi Münzenberg wrote to a friend at the Communist International in Moscow on 12 June 1933. He said: 'As a result of our persistent efforts, and after overcoming many difficulties, we have succeeded in recruiting some of the best lawyers for our plan.' He added that now a decision would have to be made as to when this panel of lawyers would meet, and who would be in charge. Münzenberg suggested forming a panel consisting of two KPD members as well as himself as the leader in order to 'organise and carry out this trial'. He added: 'The expenses will be considerable, but in my opinion this is the most effective action to counter the fascist trial.' One of the many peculiarities in the criminal case of the Reichstag fire was the fact that two trials took place almost simultaneously, with opposing outcomes: the official trial at the German Supreme Court in Leipzig and the 'counter trial' in London, in reality a hearing in front of an unofficial panel of well-known lawyers.[50]

The outcome of the proceedings in Germany was negative for the Hitler government, while the spectacle in London, carefully staged by the exiled KPD, was the propaganda success Münzenberg had hoped for. The public 'counter trial', which took place in London from 14 to 18 September, was based on the *Braunbuch*, which had opportunely been published in several languages in the summer of 1933. In the heated atmosphere just days before the official trial against van der Lubbe, Torgler and the three Bulgarians Taneff, Popoff and Dimitroff, this fact did not stand out at first. The panel consisted of eight renowned lawyers from seven different countries, including one woman, Betsy Bakker-Nort from the Netherlands. All were of good repute and had no visible connection to communism. Led by the British Attorney General Denis Nowell Pritt, the panel members reviewed documents and interviewed witnesses, including Dimitroff's sister and exiled German social democrats and communists. Wilhelm Koenen, the KPD member who had been with Ernst Torgler on the evening of the fire, also testified. In addition, the 'Oberfohren-memorandum' was read out. Although Rudolf Breitscheid, the former SPD party leader who had fled Berlin on 13 March 1933, questioned whether the document had been written by Oberfohren, he speculated that the memorandum more or less reflected his views. However, the panel in London did not go into detail – as the trial was to take place over just four days, there was no time or opportunity to carefully weigh up the evidence, as would be the case in court.

There was also no need for that, as the verdict was a foregone conclusion. This is evident from the coverage in American newspapers, as well as the wording in the preliminary 'Report of the International Advisory Panel', which was published just two days after the proceedings, on 20 September. Just one day into the 'trial', the *Chicago Daily Tribune* reported that the panel of international lawyers would 'find the Nazis guilty'. The *New York Times* reported: 'The Nazis are preparing to bring charges against the communists in Leipzig this week, while investigators outside of Germany are charging the Nazis with the arson attack.' Indeed, the 'counter trial' was designed to conclude before the Leipzig trial started, as the verdict included the findings that 'van der Lubbe is not a member, but an opponent of the communist party', that 'the documents and testimonies, as well as further evidence that the panel holds, are sufficient to determine that van der Lubbe cannot have carried out the crime on his own', and that 'the Reichstag was set on fire by leading members of the NSDAP or at their behest'.[51]

The propagandistic groundwork for the trial in Leipzig was thus laid. On 31 September 1933, all seats were taken in the largest hall of the Supreme Court. More than 100 members of the international press had been issued permits, yet only eighty-two received access cards. The *Manchester Guardian* was among those who missed out, although the newspaper had been banned in Germany since the end of April in any case. The fourth criminal division was led by Wilhelm Bünger, a well-known DVP politician [*Deutsche Volkspartei*; German People's Party] and former Saxon minister-president, who had been promoted to the Supreme Court in 1931. Although in no way a supporter of the NSDAP, he was a loyal jurist who liked to follow the rule of law. In his short opening speech, Bünger said:

> The magnitude of the event in question has led to a storm in the international press – so much so that the passion and intensity with which it has been discussed has at times overshadowed everything else that has happened. Public opinion, whether led by favour or hatred, has frequently tried to forestall the outcome of the proceedings that are still pending [...].

The unofficial panel of lawyers ('counter trial') at work. Back row, from
left: Arthur Garfield Hays (1), Betsy Bakker-Nort, (2) Denis Nowell Pritt
(chairman) (3), Vald Huit (4) and an unknown secretary (5). (Kellerhoff archive)

However, this battle of opinion will not influence this court. The German law dictates that the subject of adjudication shall be the offence specified in the charges and apparent in the light of the outcome of the hearing. German jurisdiction will only take into consideration that which is heard in court, not any unsolicited opinions outside of it.

The *Berliner Morgenpost*, by now forcibly *gleichgeschaltet* ['co-ordinated'], reported about the first day in court: 'The focus in Leipzig is upon a big trial, the biggest trial that the highest German court of law has seen. The entire world is watching this trial.' Although formal procedure was important to Bünger and Karl Werner, the chief prosecutor, the trial was by no means in accordance with the rule of law. For instance, the defendants had been permanently kept in chains in the months running up to the trial. Even according to the code of criminal procedure at the time, this was only permissible if there was a risk of suicide or if the defendants had proven to be demonstrably violent. Torgler and the three Bulgarians were subjected to this deliberately cruel measure until 31 August, whereas van der Lubbe was even brought to the courtroom in chains. It was only then that Bünger's senate revoked the order, originally made by the investigating judge. The indictment, 235 pages long, was incredibly detailed, yet biased. Thus, while the account of van der Lubbe's life was carefully documented, the reference to his 'conspiracy' with communists in Neukölln was supported by only one unreliable testimony. Similarly, the detailed description of the way the fire had spread presented a stark contrast to the sweeping accusations levelled against the four co-defendants, while the impressive forensic work of the crime scene unit stood in contrast to the weak evidence of 'the KPD's treasonous efforts'. Only a legal positivist such as Bünger could conduct a trial on such a contradictory basis. Even though, ultimately, it was not a show trial, it was also not a fair trial. Thomas Mann was only exaggerating a little when he wrote to a friend:

What a morass, what a warning! It seems as though the most nightmarish perversion of justice in history is about to take place. All that is infamous and abominable about the German situation accumulates in this trial, which will probably take on a fatal immortality. What's more, I fear that the trial's outcome will only deepen the moral isolation that Germany finds itself in today, albeit largely unaware, with perhaps disastrous consequences.[52]

At the opening of the trial in Leipzig. The defendants van der Lubbe (with interpreter) and Torgler were seated in the middle row; Dimitroff, Taneff and Popow in the back row (the latter two with interpreters). (Kellerhoff archive)

The Reichstag fire trial was remarkable in several ways. Marinus van der Lubbe, who had been caught in the act, said very little in court, and even refused any contact with his assigned counsel – he had in fact forgone his right to legal representation, arguing: 'I do not want a defence lawyer. This is my final decision. I do not want to reconsider the matter.' Nonetheless, a great battle of words took place in the court room. Georgi Dimitroff became a formidable opponent for the prosecutors and many witnesses, whom he questioned himself; his confrontation with Göring attracted worldwide attention. The senate had moved the venue to Berlin or, to be more exact, into the budget committee's hall in the Reichstag building, on 10 October. Practically all witnesses lived in Berlin, and for visits to the crime scene the court would have had to come to the capital in any case. Thus, large parts of the trial took place only a few metres away from the burnt-out plenary chamber. On 4 November, Hermann Göring – who in the meantime had been promoted to minister-president of Prussia and Reich minister for aviation – gave evidence. Dimitroff took advantage of his right to question the witness himself, and provoked him until he gave some revealing answers:

> *Dimitroff*: Is the minister-president aware that this party, with its criminal ideology, as he calls it, rules a sixth of the earth? The Soviet Union, namely.
> *Göring*: Unfortunately!
> *Dimitroff*: The Soviet Union maintains diplomatic, political and economic relations with Germany, from which hundreds of thousands of German workers have benefited and continue to benefit. Are you aware of this? (Audience is amused.)
> *Göring*: I am aware of this. […] What Russia does, does not concern me. I only have to deal with the communist party here in Germany, and with the foreign crooks who come here to burn down the Reichstag. ('Bravo' from the audience.)

Georgi Dimitroff questioned several witnesses himself – and, faced with the threat of the gallows, used the trial for a remarkable act of self-display. (Ehemaliges Dimitroff-Museum Leipzig/Kellerhoff archive)

An on-site inspection in the Reichstag. Centre left, Ernst Torgler; centre right, Marinus van der Lubbe. (National Archives, Washington DC)

Dimitroff: Of course, they cheer. It is your right to wage war against the communist party in Germany. It is my right […] to wage war against your government – and the way in which we fight our battle is defined by our relative power, not by our …

Presiding Judge Bünger: Dimitroff, I forbid you to make communist propaganda here!

Dimitroff: He is making National Socialist propaganda! […] This Bolshevik ideology of the Soviet Union, the largest and best country in the world, also has millions of supporters in Germany – often Germany's finest young men! (Audience is very amused.) Are you aware of this?

Göring: Now you listen! I'll tell you what the German people know! They know that you are behaving disgracefully, that you came here to set fire to the Reichstag, and now have the nerve to display such insolence in front of the German *Volk*! But I am not here to listen to your accusations!

Dimitroff: You are a witness.

Göring: In my opinion you are a criminal who should be sent to the gallows!

Presiding Judge Bünger: Dimitroff, I have told you not to make communist propaganda. […] You must not be surprised if the witness gets excited. If you have any questions, then please make sure they are factual.

Dimitroff: I am very satisfied with the minister's reply.

Presiding Judge Bünger: I am not interested in whether or not you are satisfied. I order you to stop speaking. […]

Dimitroff: I have some factual questions.

Presiding Judge Bünger: I order you to stop speaking.

Göring: Out with you, you scoundrel!

Presiding Judge Bünger: Take him away!

Dimitroff: Are you afraid of my questions, Herr Ministerpräsident?

Göring: You wait until I get my hands on you outside this court, you scoundrel![53]

Similarly noteworthy was the role of Alfons Sack, Torgler's chosen defence lawyer. Sack, a NSDAP member, cleverly presented the falsifications in the *Braunbuch* in such a way that he could not be accused of being pro-communist, yet still dedicatedly pleaded his client's case. However, like practically all those involved in the trial, he too was convinced that the Reichstag fire had been started by several people; this conviction was supported by no less than four experts.

Rather than assess the evidence without bias, all four had positively looked for evidence to support this theory in their comprehensive reports, although not one of them could offer any concrete proof.

Most honest was Franz Ritter from the *Chemische Technische Reichsanstalt* [Chemical Technical State Institute] in Berlin. After speculating about the way in which the fire could have spread, he summarised: 'As the available documents are insufficient, I cannot ascertain how the arson attack in the plenary chamber was most likely carried out.'

The expert from Halle, Wilhelm Schatz, an egotistical dilettante, played a particularly unfortunate role in the trial. During his examination, he invented stories of 'spontaneously inflammable liquids' which had been set aflame with the fire accelerant that had supposedly been distributed in the plenary chamber – and all of this, according to Schatz, had taken place at precisely the same time that van der Lubbe had been wandering around the unlit Reichstag building. This theory was based on the single fact that no traces of incendiary devices had been found. Because there was no evidence of fire accelerants, the experts were unsure about the kind, as well as the amount, that had been used – speculations ranged from 4 to more than 100 litres, and variably included petrol, spirit or petroleum. The fifth expert, a chemist named August Brüning, was unable to detect any fire accelerants in the damaged parts of the *Wandelhallen* that could still be investigated. In the burnt-out plenary chamber it was no longer possible to tell where the fire had started, or to take any samples. His report argued that the references to 'rags soaked in petrol' and 'traces' of fire accelerant were made up. However, Brüning was not asked to testify during the trial.[54]

Nonetheless, the verdict was a surprise. After more than 250 witnesses had testified, after Dimitroff's confrontation with Göring, after many confused statements, especially by Schatz, Judge Bünger delivered his judgement on 23 December 1933 – in the 'name of the

Hermann Göring, meanwhile promoted to minister of the interior in Prussia, testifies in court – in the undamaged chamber of the budget committee in the Reichstag. (Former Dimitroff–Museum Leipzig/Kellerhoff archive)

Reich', not the people: 'The defendants Torgler, Dimitroff, Popoff and Taneff are found not guilty. The defendant van der Lubbe is sentenced to death and permanent loss of civil rights for high treason in concomitance with seditious arson.' The Bulgarians' acquittal had been expected – even the prosecutor had pleaded in favour of this

Ernst Torgler (front) and Marinus van der Lubbe just moments before the
verdict was announced on 23 December 1933 in the Supreme Court in
Leipzig. (Former Dimitroff-Museum Leipzig/Kellerhoff archive)

Opposite: Joseph Goebbels, NSDAP Berlin party boss and by now also
Reich propaganda minister, also testified in the Supreme Court. (Former
Dimitroff-Museum Leipzig/Kellerhoff archive)

after hearing the evidence. However, it came as a great surprise that the former KPD leader had also been acquitted. Goebbels noted in his diary: 'Verdict in Leipzig. Lubbe death. All others, even Torgler, acquitted. That's what happens to a revolution if you put it in the hands of jurists. This court must disappear. Bring on the court for the protection of the German *Volk*.' Yet Bünger had essentially accommodated the government's expectations: in his verdict, he stated explicitly that Lubbe had had accomplices and that these must have been communists. However, it had not been Torgler or the three Bulgarians, but some other persons who had not been charged. Yet such subtle distinctions were too much for the *Völkischer Beobachter*. The NSDAP newspaper sharply criticised the 'miscarriage of justice' in Leipzig and announced that the trial was the 'final impulse to overhaul our outdated legal system'. However, the paper was pleased to report that the four acquitted defendants had been taken into 'protective custody' immediately after the judgement had been pronounced.[55]

Marinus van der Lubbe was executed by guillotine on 10 January 1934 in Leipzig. Before the execution, a Dutch ambassador had come to Berlin and pleaded for the verdict to be changed to a life sentence, but Reich President Hindenburg refused. Ernst Torgler was unlawfully held in custody until 1936; after that, he worked as a sales representative in Berlin. In mid-February 1934, Stalin granted the three Bulgarians Soviet citizenship. As a result, they were released and deported to Moscow. Dimitroff was celebrated as the 'hero of Leipzig' and promoted to general secretary of the Communist International. His fellow defendants did not fare quite so well: although Wassili Popoff became an official at the Comintern, he was forced to undergo 'self-criticism' sessions in 1936. Soon after, he was arrested by the Soviet secret service, the NKVD, and sentenced to fifteen years in prison. It was only after Stalin's death that he was allowed to return to Bulgaria. Taneff was also made an official, but he was also deported after 'self-criticism' sessions in the course of the purges of the communist party. After spending several years in a prison camp in the Arctic Circle, Taneff was set to go on a mission to Bulgaria, now allied with Hitler's Germany. However, he was found out and the former defendant in the Reichstag trial was shot in his home country.[56]

THE TURNING POINT

LEGENDS AND POLEMICS OF THE POST-WAR YEARS

In May 1945, the Reichstag was a ruin. The once proud building was now in a sorry state: burnt-out and completely wrecked. As such, it blended into its surroundings – the former government district was one of the most devastated areas in Germany. There was practically no trace of the repairs that had been carried out in 1933. This second destruction of the parliament building was also directly connected to the fire: while *Wehrmacht* soldiers and foreign SS-volunteers – the government district's last defence – were simply grateful for the building's solid structure, the attacking Red Army perceived the Reichstag as a symbol. More than 2,000 Soviet soldiers died in the final battle for Berlin, which raged by the Spree riverbank for forty-eight hours. Many survivors carved graffitis into the soot-blackened walls afterwards. A certain Captain Kokjuschkin and Lieutenant Krasnikow, for instance, scribbled on a wall near the south-western staircase: 'We made it to the Reichstag, Hitler's lair!'

Captain Katnikov wrote the words 'Disgraceful death. Hitler's hideout' in the eastern hallway. The Russian soldiers did not know that the Reichstag building had been of no importance during Hitler's rule – their only goal was for the 150th Rifle Division to raise the Red Flag there. Colonel Sintschenko, who was in command of one of the divison's regiments, recorded what the responsible political commissar had said prior to the attack: 'This is where, for all the world to see, the fascists began their bloody crusade against communism. This is where we must mark fascism's downfall.'[57]

In light of the terrible truths about the crimes committed by the regime and hundreds of thousands, if not millions, of Germans between 1933 and 1945 that came out after the forcible downfall of the Third Reich, the National Socialists' responsibility for the Reichstag fire went unquestioned. At the Nuremberg Tribunal, Hermann Göring, the main defendant, was also accused of having committed this crime. However, while he admitted to the other acts he had been charged with – even though he contested the competence of the court – he denied any involvement in the arson attack:

> It would have made no sense, and served no purpose, for me to set the Reichstag on fire. From an artistic point of view, I wasn't sorry the plenary chamber was burned down; I hoped I could build a better one. But I was very sorry to have to find a new Reich chamber.

He conceded that a campaign to arrest KPD members had already been planned, but that this had been meant to take place after the elections and had rashly been brought forward because of the Reichstag fire. However, neither the court nor the prosecutors believed Göring.

The testimony by Hans-Bernd Gisevius, one of the key witnesses, was one of the reasons why nobody doubted the Nazis' guilt. Gisevius unequivocally stated:

To put it briefly, and to keep to bare facts for now, it came to our attention that Hitler had expressed a general wish for a large propaganda coup. It was Goebbels' job to prepare some suggestions for this, and it was Goebbels who first had the idea to set the Reichstag on fire. Goebbels discussed this with the leader of the SA brigade, Karl Ernst, and suggested, in some detail, how the arson attack could take place.

Gisevius also provided detailed information about the supposed development of the arson attack:

A certain tincture was chosen, one that every pyrotechnician knows. It needs to be sprayed onto a surface and then it ignites after a certain amount of time, after hours or minutes. The building was accessed via a passageway that runs between the Palais and the Reichstag building. Ten reliable SA men were organised, and then Göring was informed of the plan, which is why, as it happens, he did not give an election speech on that particular evening, but instead was to be found at his desk at the interior ministry in Berlin. Göring was expected to intentionally mislead the police in the first instance, to which he agreed. The plan was to pin the blame for the fire on the communists from the very beginning – this was also the brief those ten SA men, who were to carry out the crime, had been given.

Gisevius still had more to say:

As to how we came about this information, I can only add that one of the ten men who sprayed the tincture was a notorious criminal. Six months after the event, he was excluded from the SA. When he did not receive the reward he had been promised, he felt compelled to report his knowledge to the Supreme Court, which was based in Leipzig at the time. He was shown to a coroner, who put it on record. However, the Gestapo found out about this and the letter to the Supreme Court was intercepted and destroyed.

And the SA man who had revealed the information, he was called Rall, was dastardly murdered with Göring's full knowledge and by order of Gestapo Chief Diels. When we found his body, that put us on the right track.

At this point Judge Jackson asked: 'What happened to the ten SA men who set the Reichstag on fire? Are any of them still alive?' Gisevius replied: 'As far as we're aware, none of them are alive today. Most were killed on 30 June 1934 during the Night of the Long Knives. Only one man, a certain Heini Gewähr, joined the police force, but he was killed on the eastern front during the war.'[58]

In the light of such an emphatic statement, there were few who, in the post-war years, doubted that the Nazis were the culprits. Nobody noticed that the 'key witness' had his own agenda. In June 1933, the young Gisevius had just received his doctorate in law and had switched from the DNVP to the NSDAP. The *Völkischer Beobachter* had even explicitly reported this under the headline 'DNVP Leaders Join the National Socialist Fold'. After this, Gisevius found employment with the Prussian secret state police, the precursor of the Gestapo, where he worked his way up to head of division. However, already at this point he attracted negative attention. The first Gestapo Chief, Rudolf Diels, for instance, called him a 'scheming careerist' and a 'tattletale who was obliging to everyone able to further his career'. Apparently, Gisevius had tried to get rid of his rival Diels with a smear campaign, claiming he was a 'covert communist'. When this failed, he moved to the interior ministry, and later into the private sector. During the war, Gisevius was employed as the German vice consul in Zurich. While he was there, he colluded with Allen Dulles, the chief of the US secret service in Switzerland. He was also in contact with the German resistance movement within the *Wehrmacht*, although he was not part of the inner circle; he acted mainly as a courier into neutral Switzerland. On 20 July 1944, when Claus Graf Stauffenberg was still desperately trying to organise a coup, despite the failed assassination of the 'Führer', Givesius was, by his own account, in the Bendlerblock building in Berlin.

However, it has never been possible to determine how much of this generously embellished statement corresponds to the truth. His claim that Stauffenberg harboured 'eastern sympathies', as he had tried to warn Dulles, was certainly implausible. Yet his information earned him the status of 'key witness' in Nuremberg – and thus the celebrity status that had so far eluded him. However, Ernst Torgler dismissed Gisevius as someone who 'pretends to have been present all the time, when in fact his knowledge is based only on hearsay, or, at best, on the Gestapo files he studied'. He had no time for his revelations: 'All these claims in Gisevius' book are malicious lies or at least silly, careless gossip.' Indeed, Givesius' testimony was entirely made up; the alleged accomplice Adolf Rall, for instance, was in protective custody in Berlin-Moabit on 27 February 1933, and would therefore not have been able to spray a 'tincture' in the parliament building.[59]

Thus, an element of doubt about the Nazis' responsibility for the Reichstag fire remained. These doubts grew when Rudolf Diels published his memoirs in 1950. Of course, the first Gestapo chief, who was dismissed in 1934, was keen to whitewash his own role. Yet the vehemence with which he denied the earlier claim that communists had been involved in the arson attack was surprising: 'I was convinced that it was the National Socialists who set the Reichstag on fire, from just a few weeks after the fire, until 1945. I don't believe that any more.' Faced with this contradiction, the Federal Agency for Homeland Services (now Federal Agency for Civic Education) commissioned the historian Richard Wolff to prepare a report about the Reichstag fire. His twenty-six-page report, in addition to six documents relating to the fire, was published in early 1956, in the supplement of Bonn's official weekly paper *Das Parlament*. His conclusion was clear: 'It has been proven that van der Lubbe set fire to the Reichstag with wholly inadequate means.

At the same time, and as the result of careful planning, others were busy setting fire to the Reichstag, especially the plenary chamber, thoroughly destroying it. These others were not communists, but National Socialists.' However, Wolff's report did not clarify the debate, as the agency had hoped – the report was surprisingly amateurish. Thus, Wolff lamented the 'astonishing lack of sources'; he had been unable, for example, to obtain an official shorthand report of the chief prosecutor's charge and the proceedings. Likewise, it had been impossible to find any of the seven copies of van der Lubbe's interrogation records. In addition, Wolff declared: 'On 28 February, that is, when the arson attack was first reported, the German press had already practically been gagged.' Wolff had been in contact with some of the policemen who had been involved in the investigation, but had not been able to obtain the information he had hoped for. He concluded that the witnesses, 'against their better judgement or for other reasons that are not entirely clear, use their knowledge to play havoc with public opinion'. Wolff also declared the 'Oberfohren-memorandum' to be genuine.

In reality, it has been possible to access the indictment, the trial's transcript and the verdict without difficulty from as early as the mid-1950s. Moreover, the bourgeois German newspapers, although already browbeaten by the Nazis by late February and early March 1933, especially in Berlin, were only truly 'co-ordinated' in the following weeks. By 1955/56, several of the investigators involved in the case were willing to comment; some had already done so, occasionally using a pseudonym. However, they categorically refused to be abused for a 'trial' where the verdict – that van der Lubbe had been a 'tool' of the NSDAP – was clear from the outset. The 'Oberfohren-memorandum', meanwhile, had already been exposed as a fake during the Reichstag fire trial. It comes as no great surprise, then, that Rudolf Diels sharply ridiculed Wolff's 'report', and his refusal to accept the simple truth that the Dutch communist had acted alone:

Even if a demigod were to present conclusive evidence to prove that the Nazis – despite their criminal nature – were not involved in the Reichstag fire, public opinion would still, for reasons of political sensitivity, conceal the truth, or accuse the archangel of being a neo-fascist.[60]

At the same time as Wolff, another man was working on the subject of the Reichstag fire. Born in 1912, Fritz Tobias was a bookseller, but from 1946 worked in various roles in the Lower Saxon public service. In 1933, he had lost his 'status, job and home' as an 'indirect result of the Reichstag fire'. The same happened to his father, who was also a social democrat. For Tobias, it was obvious that the new rulers had set fire to the Reichstag themselves. He said: 'Like many other sceptics, I hoped to learn the carefully guarded truth about the fire after the collapse of the Third Reich. There were some revelations, yet no matter how patiently I waited, year after year, the truth about the Reichstag fire never materialised.' Instead, he came into contact with Ernst Torgler and Walter Zirpins, a former chief inspector involved in the inquiry against van der Lubbe, and later head of the criminal investigation department in Hanover. Both men were of the opinion that van der Lubbe had acted alone. Tobias systematically began to collect information about the Reichstag fire. As Wolff's report had been so unsatisfactory, Paul Franken, director of the Federal Agency, encouraged Tobias to publish his research. At a later date, he emphatically stated: 'Of course I am willing to confirm that, after Wolff's unfortunate report, I encouraged, or virtually prompted you to carry out your research regarding the Reichstag fire. For me as a historian the main priority is to uncover the truth.' Franken added: 'Our discussions were such that I have no objections to you telling third parties that you carried out your research "at the instigation of or at the request of the Federal Agency for Civic Education".'[61]

The initial result was a series of sensational articles in the weekly magazine *Der Spiegel* towards the end of 1959 and in early 1960, entitled

'Stand up, van der Lubbe!' Two journalists – first freelance writer Paul Karl Schmidt, and then editor Günther Zacharias – had written the series based on Tobias' manuscript. Paul Karl Schmidt had been press chief at the foreign office from 1940, and had occasionally written nasty anti-semitic file notes. However, as they were not made public after the war, he was able to establish a career in journalism – at the publishing house Springer Verlag, and also the *Spiegel*. Using the pseudonym 'Paul Carrell', he also became a successful author, mainly with books about the *Wehrmacht*. However, 'Carrell' was not enthusiastic about the Reichstag fire series:

> He really took his time editing it – so much so that Tobias wanted to end the collaboration with the *Spiegel*. He was so disappointed with Schmidt's work ('factual mistakes en masse') that he sent pages and pages of corrections to the magazine. From then on, Günther Zacharias took over as editor of Tobias' Reichstag fire series.

The series was an instant sensation, but was predominantly met with scepticism. The *Spiegel* received scores of readers' letters. A representative survey carried out by the Allensbach Institute showed that 37 per cent of Germans interviewed still held the National Socialists responsible, 8 per cent the KPD and only 6 per cent Marinus van der Lubbe. A quarter of those surveyed were unsure, and 20 per cent had never heard of the Reichstag fire – however, this applied mainly to those aged 16 to 29. The foreign press also reported on Tobias' series, though for the most part it was sceptical or deprecating.[62]

The Hamburg weekly paper *Die Zeit*, whose editorial office were located in the same building as the *Spiegel* at the time, reacted even more critically. Hans-Bernd Gisevius, of all people, responded with a four-part series entitled 'The Reichstag Fire: A Distorted Picture'. Once again Gisevius, the former head of division at the Gestapo, accused SA man Hans-Georg Gewehr of having led the arson attack. However, while at the Nuremberg trial Gisevius had claimed that 'Heini Gewähr' had been killed on the eastern front, he now said that the alleged arsonist lived in Düsseldorf as a building contractor. As a result of Gisevius' articles, the public prosecution service initiated a preliminary investigation against Gewehr for arson; orders for his company were cancelled. In January 1962, criminal proceedings were suspended as no probable cause could be established, but by then Gewehr had left the company's management team. Gewehr now sued Gisevius and, by 1966, won on three different court levels. Gisevius was no longer allowed to claim that Gewehr had been involved in the arson attack. However, as the judges did not want to stifle the debate, they also ruled that articles on the subject could still be published, as long as Hans-Georg Gewehr's 'honour' was protected. After further lawsuits, he was also awarded damages. Gisevius, meanwhile, having been found guilty of lying, was 'financially ruined'.[63]

Tobias turned the manuscript that had served as the basis for the *Spiegel* series into a thick book. Published in 1961, it contained, among others, serious accusations against Hans-Bernd Gisevius, claiming that his 'allegedly personal experiences regarding the Reichstag fire' had been revealed as 'ranging from illogical to downright nonsense, and from being incredible to verifiably untrue'. Gisevius sued and obtained an interim order against the book's publication. However, this order was lifted during the main trial: the publication of Tobias' book was permitted and Gisevius had to bear the costs of the trial. The book, all 723 pages of it, was no bestseller, though – the German version was never reprinted after the first edition, and only one English translation was published. Perhaps the audience was already too familiar with Fritz Tobias' findings, which had taken up 107 pages in the *Spiegel* series. Moreover, while the volume did feature a comprehensive appendix containing hitherto unpublished sources, including van der Lubbe's supposedly missing interrogation records, it did not include a reference list. Thus, Tobias was easy prey for many critics, who dismissed the achievements of this 'amateur historian'.

Occasionally, Tobias did go a little too far. For instance, he pointedly wrote: 'In humankind's moment of glory, in the blazing symbol of the defeated Weimar Republic, the civil Reich chancellor turned into the dictator Adolf Hitler, inebriated with power and with a fantastical sense of mission.' It is true that the night of the Reichstag fire had brought further radicalisation, perhaps prompted by Hitler's fear that the supposedly communist arsonists could still thwart his plans to take over power in Germany. However, even before the fire he had hardly been a normal, that is 'civil', chancellor, but instead a ruthless ideologue. Yet despite the book's weaknesses, Tobias – a senior civil servant from Hanover who had not studied history – had set the scholars a difficult task: now it was up to them to independently verify his findings.[64]

First in line for this task was the Munich *Institut für Zeitgeschichte*. Already in 1960, Martin Broszat had published a 'general discussion' about the Reichstag fire in the academic journal *Vierteljahrshefte für Zeitgeschichte*, in which he argued that, regardless of who was guilty, it is clear that Hitler and his supporters had 'cleverly and immediately' used the arson attack to their advantage. He added that the contentious efforts to assign blame were 'less about the revision of facts that may be crucial for the historical verdict, and more about a case that causes a stir because it has reached symbolic meaning in contemporary public consciousness'. In view of this, he argued that 'professional' contemporary historians should not shy away from carrying out criminological investigations. However, Broszat conceded that historians would occasionally 'reach the limits of their profession', as they would simply not be able to conduct a full criminal investigation.

As a result, the institute's director, Helmut Krausnick, commissioned senior teacher Hans Schneider to carry out a critical study of Tobias' book, to be published in the *Vierteljahrshefte*. It took Schneider until 1962 to deliver a lengthy draft, which the institute, rightly, deemed 'unsuitable for publication'. Instead, the historian Hans Mommsen wrote a comprehensive report on Tobias' theses, which was published in the *Vierteljahrshefte* in 1964. Mommsen's study rested on three main arguments. First, he demonstrated that the claim of it having been a group of perpetrators who set the Reichstag on fire was merely a hypothesis. There had never been a single piece of concrete evidence to support this theory; it had been based solely on rumours and presumptions. However, these had always been vehemently denied by van der Lubbe. Second, Mommsen reassessed the plausibility of the fire experts' reports. It was not even necessary for him to consider criminological or pyrotechnical details, as the experts' reports and testimonies in court were contradictory. Finally, Mommsen turned his attention to the political consequences of the Reichstag fire and showed that the Hitler government's reaction had been chaotic, rather than well-prepared. He concluded: 'The study that we conducted, and which would not have been possible without Fritz Tobias' research, largely confirms Tobias' findings. Further, when considered from a political point of view, an involvement by the National Socialists in van der Lubbe's arson attack can be ruled out.' The *Spiegel* aptly summarised Mommsen's paper in one sentence: 'This academic essay spells triumph for Tobias, as it awards his research scholarly recognition.' However, the debate about the Reichstag fire was far from over.[65]

8

THE COUNTERFEITERS

THE 'LUXEMBOURG COMMITTEE' AND ITS PURPORTED DOCUMENTS

Just before Christmas, on 23 December 1966, the headline of a full-page article in the Berlin daily newspaper *Telegraf* announced a sensation: 'The Reichstag Fire in an Entirely New Light.' The subtitle claimed: 'Recently discovered documents indict Nazis'. The article promised a 'sensational turning point: a man is in possession of new, hitherto undiscovered secret documents, with which he wants to prove that the Nazis planned and carried out the arson attack. The *Telegraf* spoke with the man – the outcome of this conversation amounts to more than just a news item.' The key witness in question was Edouard Calic, 'originally a lawyer, and now living in Berlin, working as a correspondent for French newspapers'. The article claimed that Calic 'had been able to add documents that had been found by the Soviets in Germany, and sent via Bulgaria, to his already existing collection of material and testimonies'. The most important piece of evidence mentioned in the *Telegraf* article was a quotation attributed to Hitler: 'The faster this gossip chamber is burnt down, the sooner the German *Volk* will be free of foreign influences.' Apparently, the NSDAP chief had said this to Richard Breiting, a journalist from Leipzig, on 4 May 1931, almost two years before the arson attack. Breiting had recorded this in his notes, and these were now being quoted for the first time. Moreover, Calic put forward eleven further hypotheses which, so he claimed, proved that the Nazis were responsible for the Reichstag fire. However, these were only briefly touched on in the *Telegraf* article.

The article was part of a campaign that Calic had initiated in France a few months earlier. He had made his debut as a historian in the autumn of 1966, with the book *Himmler et son Empire* [*Himmler and his Empire*]; it was never published in German. Instead, he published the volume *Ohne Maske. Hitler-Breiting Geheimgespräche 1931* [*Without a Mask. The Secret Hitler-Breiting Conversations of 1931*] with a prestigious publishing house in Frankfurt two years later, at the end of 1968. It contained the minutes of two meetings between the NSDAP chief and the former editor-in-chief of the daily newspaper *Leipziger Neuesten Nachrichten*. It was here that the quotation, already published in the article eighteen months earlier, was now published in context:

> The Reichstag is an extremely ugly building, a meeting place, a gossip chamber for the representatives of the putrid bourgeoisie and the seduced working masses. The building, as well as the institution that it houses, are a disgrace for the German *Volk*. They must disappear some day. I say: the faster this gossip chamber is burnt down, the sooner the German *Volk* will be free of foreign influences. I can assure you of one thing, Mr Breiting – I will never set foot in this house of traitors.

However, the publication of the full quotation had the effect of calling the source's reliability into question – while it was well known that Hitler had despised parliamentarianism, it was also known that the NSDAP chief had wanted to keep the Reichstag as a (naturally powerless) 'German institution', as well as the Paul Wallot buildings. At the height of his power, Hitler even decided that the building would remain where it was when Berlin was turned into the world capital 'Germania' – a project which otherwise envisaged major rebuilding work, especially in the area around the bend in the Spree river called the 'Spreebogen'. Although not a reliable witness, Hitler's favourite architect Albert Speer described how the 'Führer' had wanted to renovate the building and turn the plenary chamber into a library, against Speer's advice.[66]

Nonetheless, *Ohne Maske* had positive reviews at first. Sebastian Haffner, the well-known publicist, for instance, described the book as a 'first-class historical document'. The minutes published in the volume seemed to confirm many details that were already known from other sources – for instance from *Mein Kampf* [*My Struggle*] or Hermann Rauschning's *Gespräche mit Hitler* [*Hitler Speaks*]. According to Calic, a renowned handwriting expert had certified the printed version: 'The transcriptions correspond to the original documents.' However, the quoted report does not contain this sentence by Hitler. With time, it became clear that the scepticism that had been voiced about Hitler's purported quotation about the Reichstag had to be extended to Calic's entire volume. A witness who had been present at, and heard, the actual conversation between the NSDAP leader and the national-liberal editor-in-chief had said shortly after the book's publication: 'The first conversation is, for the most part, made up; the second conversation never took place.' He added that Breiting had not taken down the conversation in shorthand. In 1972, the well-known British historian Hugh Trevor-Roper was surprised that Hitler was said to have despised the Reichstag building so much.

Seven years later, Karl-Heinz Janßen, a journalist at *Die Zeit*, detected linguistic discrepancies in the 'secret conversations'. His analysis of the supposed minutes showed that both Hitler and Breiting were using phrases that were literal translations from Serbo-Croatian, Calic's mother tongue – for instance the term 'Diskretionsrecht' (Serbo-Croation: 'diskreciono pravo') instead of the German term 'Ermessungsspielraum', 'Domination der Meere' ('dominacija morima') instead of the German word 'Seeherrschaft', or 'Militärstreich' ('vojni udar') instead of the commonly used German term 'Militärputsch'. Janßen concluded: 'Edouard Calic's book *Ohne Maske* is one of the most audacious historical misrepresentations of this century.' The book's publisher sued, but lost on two different court levels. Calic claimed to have come across the shorthand texts in Breiting's estate in Leipzig – a productive 'source', as will be seen. However, Calic was unable to produce any original documents; he said the Iron Curtain meant they were inaccessible. Although this changed when Germany was reunited in 1990, the alleged Breiting shorthand texts have still not surfaced. However, in 1999, an essay appeared that claimed that records held by the East German secret police could prove that 'documents from the Leipzig editor-in-chief Richard Breiting's estate had indeed been handed over by the inheritors'. However, there was no shelf mark for these records.[67]

Calic's personal background alone was questionable. In 1984, the superior court of justice rejected Calic's appeal, partly for this reason:

> The depiction of the claimant as a shady character is a value judgement. This assessment of the claimant is covered by the right of free speech pursuant to Art.5 sub-clause 1 sentence 1 of the German *Grundgesetz* [Basic Law] and the right of free press pursuant to Art. 5 sub-clause 1 sentence 2 – in which the defendant as part of the press also participates – since the limits set by those basic rights have not been exceeded by the criticism of the plaintiff's person chosen by the defendant.

Calic, born in 1910, had worked as a foreign correspondent in Berlin for a small newspaper in Zagreb from 1939. In March 1943, he was listed as a member of the foreign press in the Berlin telephone directory. Despite this, Calic claimed during the debate that he had been banned from his profession by the Gestapo in 1941, and that in 1942 he had been arrested and taken to the Sachsenhausen concentration camp. Calic reappeared in the summer of 1945, moved to Paris and then returned to West Berlin towards the end of the 1950s. Because he had spent time in a concentration camp, Calic assumed that he would be considered a trustworthy researcher of the National Socialist era. In 1969, he explained how he had come across the subject of the Reichstag fire. He said that in Sachsenhausen he had acquired a document by Eduard Wagner, a quartermaster general of the *Wehrmacht*. This document, he continued, had proven that the resistance movement of 20 July had planned to announce that the Nazis were the instigators of the Reichstag fire after the removal of Hitler. Wagner, a co-conspirator, had tried to commit suicide after the failed assassination attempt on 20 July 1944, and had been brought to Sachsenhausen badly injured. Here, he was 'operated to death' by a SS doctor. However, Calic claimed that a group of prisoners had got hold of Wagner's dossier, who had then passed it onto him. As a matter of fact, Wagner had committed suicide by a shot to the head on 23 July 1944, at exacty 12.41 p.m., and had never set foot in Sachsenhausen.[68]

In 1968, a new institution with the sole purpose of investigating the Reichstag fire was founded. Its first planned name, the 'Committee for the Investigation of the Instigation of the Reichstag Fire', was changed to 'International Committee for Scholarly Research on the Causes and Consequences of the Second World War' after Hans Mommsen pointed out to Edouard Calic, the incoming committee secretary general, during a meeting in Essen that it was 'potentially too biased'. Several leading figures gave their support to the committee, from Willy Brandt [former West German chancellor] to Eugen Kogon [historian and Holocaust survivor], to *Telegraf* publisher Arno Scholz. The unprofessional approach displayed by the committee's spokesperson, the Swiss historian Walther Hofer, did not put them off. For instance, in a letter to the Lower Saxon Interior Minister, Richard Lehners, Hofer accused Fritz Tobias of 'blackmail' and of 'systematically thwarting a scientific project' and demanded 'disciplinary action'. However, Lehners recommended that Hofer seek recourse to the courts. He added: 'I recommend, in your own interest, to refrain from making such defamatory remarks about Ministerial Counsellor [*Ministerialrat*] Tobias until you can prove your accusations are correct.'

The institute, dominated by Calic, became known as the 'Luxembourg Committee'. It was financed, at least in part, by German tax revenues. Its main output was in the form of two *Dokumentation* [reports], which aimed to prove the Nazis' responsibility for the arson attack. The first volume, published in 1972, contained the 'negative proof' that Marinus van der Lubbe could not have set fire to the building by himself, according to the editors, which included Hofer and Calic. 'Positive proof' of the Nazis' guilt was then delivered in the second volume, released in 1978. The third volume, supposedly 'ready to go to print' that same year, was never published; its planned content was 'the motivation for and findings of the Reichstag fire from the perspective of the witnesses and experts'.[69]

However, these volumes were not scientific reports, but instead compilations that had been put together somewhat randomly. For instance, the first volume contained a complex report about the fire in the plenary chamber, excerpts from the trial records (including the fire experts' reports), as well as firemen's testimonies that had been recorded between 1960 and 1971. Just two weeks after the volume's publication in July 1972, however, its distribution had to be stopped. It turned out that the editors had wrongly claimed that *Spiegel* journalist Günther Zacharias had been a member of the NSDAP. In actual fact, Zacharias was only 11 years old in 1935, the year he was supposed to have joined Hitler's party. The second volume contained another – though this time coherent – account of the supposed spread of the fire, as well as several texts containing hundreds of quotations which reiterated the claims of Münzensberg's campaign in 1933, but which had long been refuted. More importantly, the appendix included about half a dozen documents which contained sensational information – details that were not recorded anywhere else, but that served to confirm each other. Apparently this was supposed to make the texts appear genuine; in fact, this congruence only showed that they had all been written by the same author, and were therefore fake. It was not possible to say for certain who had composed these fake 'sources'. Officially, Hofer and his colleague Christoph Graf assumed responsibility – even before the second volume was published they had already introduced themselves with the article 'The Reichstag Fire: New Sources' in a scientific journal. In the article, they wrote: 'Professor Edouard Calic in particular has worked tirelessly over the past years to locate and collect private sources.' About half the documents were said to have come from Breiting's estate in Leipzig – the same source, that is, where Calic had supposedly found the 'secret conversations'.[70]

It was obvious that the documents in the appendix of the Reichstag fire 'Dokumentation' were fake. Oddly, they all had one thing in common: none of them were accessible to serious researchers, because they were either based on 'reliable witness statements', only existed in the form of transcripts or were not available for scrutiny for a number of other reasons. In addition, all the witnesses were dead by the time their supposed testimonies were published for the first time. Lastly, almost all the statements were only published in fragments, and had not been properly edited. In court, any of these points would have been enough to reject them as pieces of evidence.

An examination of the report's content led to a similar conclusion. The 'K-documents', for instance, had supposedly been written by

Eugen von Kessel, a former member of the *Freikorps* [German volunteer unit], who had been killed by the SS on 30 June 1934. These records contained a mix of notes, comments and reports, including information about a meeting between Göring and a few confidants in the Reich chancellery on 23 March 1933. Apparently, Göring had said to Karl Ernst, the SA leader:

> The lads did a very good job. It's disgraceful that they were nearly caught by the police and fire brigade, that lot infected by Marxism. Every corner of that joint should have gone up in flames. If Gempp's people hadn't been so overeager, they could have finished the job. The Young Turks were luckier when they burned down Ciragan Palace, and I bet they didn't use an underground heating duct.

Practically none of these details corresponded to the truth. Not even Göring would have dared to talk like that in the Reich chancellery – many of the long-serving civil servants who had not yet been 'brought into line' still worked in the building in March 1933. It would have been an incalculable risk to openly make such a statement there. The supposed date was also incorrect: on 23 March 1933, the Enabling Act was being passed in the Reichstag, and Göring, as president of the Reichstag, had spent most of the day in the Kroll opera house opposite the Wallot building, which was being used as the government's temporary seat. Is it really likely that he would have scheduled a meeting with his team of arsonists on that very day? The wording also raises doubts. While Göring was known to consider the Prussian police as 'infected by Marxism', he had never accused the Berlin fire brigade – Fire Chief Gempp's 'people' – of the same. It is also unlikely that Göring would have described SA men as 'lads' or 'guys'. Lastly, the 'Young Turks', a nationalist movement that had ruled the Ottoman Empire from 1908, had not 'burned down'

Ciragan Palace; an explosion in one of the central heating vents had caused the fire on 19 January 1910. Only its outside shell was left standing.

It was relatively easy to find the source of inspiration for the 'K-documents'. A book by Hermann Rauschning entitled *Gespräche mit Hitler* [*Conversations with Hitler*], published in Zurich in 1940, contained a passage about comments that Göring was supposed to have made in an anteroom of Hitler's office in the Reich chancellery 'shortly after the Reichstag fire'. Among other things, he is said to have imparted 'details about the Reichstag fire' to Himmler, Frick and a few *Gauleiter* from western Germany. Rauschning wrote: 'I only learned from this conversation that the National Socialist leadership had sole responsibility for the Reichstag fire.' When Göring, the main defendant in the Nuremberg trials in 1946, was asked to comment on this extract specifically, he said:

> I know that Mr Rauschning claims to have spoken to me about this in his book, which has been referenced several times. I only met Mr Rauschning twice in my life, and only very briefly. If I had set fire to the Reichstag, then I would presumably only have told my closest confidants, if anyone at all. I would never have told a man I didn't know at all and who I would not even be able to describe today.[71]

It was even easier to prove that another document, a supposed statement by Paul Löbe, the long-standing president of the Reichstag, had been faked. According to this document in the Hofer-Calic 'Dokumentation', supposedly composed on the thirtieth anniversary of the fire, the SPD politician is said to have declared:

> I was in Breslau on the night of the Reichstag fire. When I returned to Berlin, I closely examined the small burn marks and the devastation of

the plenary chamber. I was shown around by Galle, the director of the Reichstag [...] Galle said he was relieved that the three thousand books in the library had been spared by the flames. Göring hadn't dared to go that far. At that time we had several pieces of evidence to suggest it was the National Socialists. One of our sources was said director of the Reichstag [...] A further source was Gempp, Berlin's fire chief, who confirmed that the arsonists had gained access through the underground tunnel. He said that he and his men had come across traces of liquid fire accelerant everywhere.

However, Paul Löbe did not know any of this in 1959. In a reader's letter, he wrote: 'Even later on I remained unaware of the details.' He had written the letter in response to the comprehensive *Spiegel* series about the Reichstag fire. After this, Paul Löbe never again said or wrote anything about the Reichstag fire until he died in 1967. Yet in 1978, the appendix to the second volume of the 'Dokumentation' contained his supposed statement from 1963 – however, only in the form of a transcript from 1971. This in itself suggested that this 'source' was wholly unreliable; an examination of the content confirms that Löbe cannot have been the author of this 'statement'. For in that case the social democrat would have had to have made a mistake when it came to the parliament's gem: the library. In the 'statement' from 1963, it said that at least the 'three thousand books in the library' had been spared. In reality, the library contained 300,000 books – a figure that Löbe was well aware of. It was impossible that he would have made such a mistake. Finally, it was inconceivable that Löbe, vice president of the Reichstag at the time, would have said to have been relieved that Göring 'hadn't dared' to destroy the library. Just days after the fire, many social democrats and communists had been persecuted and brutalised by SA men. However much the 300,000 books may have meant to Löbe, their meaning pales into insignificance in comparison to these crimes committed at the end of February and early March 1933 – crimes where Göring had 'dared to go that far'. It was also possible to identify the probable source for Löbe's statement: in his memoirs of 1954, based on what he had read in the *Braunbuch*, the social democrat still maintained that it was the Nazis who had set fire to the Reichstag. However, when the *Spiegel* series presented a different point of view, Löbe evidently changed his opinion, and wrote a letter to the magazine.[72]

The two reports published by the 'Luxembourg Committee' were received with great interest by both the public and academics. The reports also sparked a heated media debate between *Die Zeit* and the *Tagesspiegel*. While the Hamburg-based weekly newspaper and its historical editor Karl-Heinz Janßen launched a campaign against Calic and Hofer, the daily Berlin newspaper printed articles in support of the counterfeiters. These were written by Jürgen Schmädecke, a former *Tagesspiegel* journalist, who now worked for the Berlin historical commission. However, nothing truly new was published; the same applied to the fiftieth anniversary in 1983. In the same year, the controversy reached a new low point when a brief letter by Walther Hofer was printed in the *Historische Zeitschrift*. Hofer had replied to a scathing review of the second volume of the 'Dokumentation', in which Hans Mommsen had written: 'As the committee rejects the plausible answer that it was a single perpetrator whose crime was subsequently exploited by the regime, it gets tangled up in a complex assortment of dubious alternative versions and secondary hypotheses, which is why the book turns out to be virtually unreadable.' Mommsen further demanded that the 'so-called "original documents"' mentioned in the appendix – the book's key section – were produced. Hofer responded by claiming that this demand was an 'unprecedented insult' that he had 'never encountered in the history of his profession'. He argued that it was 'incomprehensible' that sceptics should regard the 'documents' in the appendix as 'dubious'. However, quite the opposite was the case: any historian would think it wholly unreasonable that Hofer refused to produce the key sources to verify his claims.[73]

In 1986, fuel was added to the fire when six historians and journalists – including Janßen, Mommsen and Tobias – launched a polemic attack on the 'Luxembourg Committee'. They demonstrated that the 'Dokumentation' contained dozens of errors. Their book was conceived as a polemic, and as such it fulfilled its objective. Walther Hofer's response to the accusations was printed on the flyer for the book launch:

> The only purpose of this new publication is to discredit our sound documentary evidence that shows that the National Socialists were responsible for the Reichstag fire in 1933, and as a result to revive the legend of Marinus van der Lubbe as the sole perpetrator and the National Socialists' innocence, which has long been refuted.

However, at the same time, Hofer ventured out of cover, which he had not been willing to do three years earlier:

> The signatories do not need to take back a single word or document in the 'Dokumentation' in question. They also in no way shy away from having these documents verified by a genuinely neutral and trustworthy body. They have only refused to produce the documents to the authors of the most recent pamphlet.

After this announcement, Hofer had no choice but to present the 'documents' in question to an independent institution for scrutiny. Until then, nobody outside of Calic's close circle had seen the documents; it was the abbreviated version included in the second volume of the 'Dokumentation' that had served as the basis for repeated criticism. Now, Calic signed a contract with the federal archive in Coblenz. In 1983, it had taken the archive's experts only a few days to expose the 'Hitler diaries' as a hoax. Forty-five documents were submitted to the archive, although most were transcripts or photocopies. When challenged, Christoph Graf said the archive had unsuccessfully searched for the originals. He added that, from now on, it would be 'assumed that the originals were non-existent'. Graf, Hofer's former assistant, was unaware of the deeper meaning implied by this sub-clause – there had, of course, never been any 'originals', as they had been faked from the start. Consequently, the documents that had been submitted to the archive were returned – it would not be possible, it was claimed, to carry out a proper examination of those documents that were only available as copies. Instead, Hans Booms, the president of the federal archive, offered to store the documents and make them available to interested scholars, but Hofer declined his offer.[74]

Hofer refused because he believed he had found another way to have the much coveted certificate of authenticity issued for the 'Dokumente': the forensic document laboratory in Zurich was willing to examine the papers. Although Graf had said that the originals were 'non-existent', one original page had appeared in the meantime. It was one page of the 'K-documents', with the page numbers nine and ten. Apart from this, the examiners in Zurich also only had copies of the documents said to be from the 1930s. Unlike the experts at the federal archive, the team in Zurich did not consider this to be a problem and readily certified that they had been unable to identify any anachronisms. However, the police laboratory did not examine the content of the documents. Hofer and his supporters nonetheless claimed that the report certified the documents' authenticity. The document laboratory had, of course, said nothing of the sort – the report merely stated that there was no evidence of physical or chemical anachronisms. The experts in Zurich had simply confirmed that the typewriters used to type these documents had been in use in the 1930s, when they were allegedly produced. This does not mean, however, that the documents were actually written during that period.

However, Hofer and his supporters had claimed victory too soon, as a further discovery by the laboratory soon put them under severe pressure. One of the original 'K-documents' bore a watermark of 1935 – yet the documents' alleged author, Eugen von Kessel, had been killed on 30 June 1934. When he was confronted, Hofer claimed that the single sheet of paper was the transcript of a shorthand note which had been made between 1935 and 1937. Until then, this had of course never been mentioned. With this, the second round of the Reichstag fire debate drew to a close. It finally ended in 1992, when Hofer-scholar Alexander Bahar published new editions of the documentary volumes of 1972 and 1978. He added a few new documents, notably the report by the police laboratory in Zurich. The book appeared in a series called *Unerwünschte Bücher zum Faschismus* [*Unwanted Books about Fascism*] published by the Freiburg-based publisher Ahriman. It would be generous to describe this publishing house as 'obscure'. The masthead of the new edition contained the interesting sentence: 'Orders received by the publisher will be processed within a week. No response proves postal censorship by Nato. In this case, resend order by registered mail – a lesson for those with a belief in liberal-democratic constitutional order or coincidence, a private lesson in civics.'[75]

9

THE CAMPAIGN

RENEWED DISPUTE ABOUT THE PERPETRATORS AND MORE ACTS OF DEFAMATION

The publication of the new edition of the 'Dokumentation' in 1992 did not cause much of a stir, and it also remained quiet on the sixtieth anniversary of the fire at the end of February 1993. The debate surrounding the criminal case of the Reichstag fire seemed to be over. However, the calm did not last long, as several new combatants were poised to enter the fray. The debate about the arson attack began anew – now in its fourth round, after those of 1933/4, 1956–64 and 1966–88. This latest row was triggered by the fact that the original documents of the preliminary investigation could now be accessed at the federal archive. Since 1945, they had been locked up in the Soviet Union. In the 1970s, they had been made available to party historians from East Germany and Bulgaria. These historians had selected 738 documents and published them in two volumes in 1982 and 1989. At the time of the first volume's release, it

125

was agreed by Anatoli Jegorow, the director of the Institute of Marxism-Leninism of the Central Committee of the Soviet Communists, and Günter Heyden, the director of the Institute of Marxism-Leninism of the Central Committee of the SED [*Sozialistische Einheitspartei Deutschlands*; Socialist Unity Party of Germany], that the Leipzig trial documents – comprising 207 files (including sixteen duplicates) and a total of 50,494 pages – should be transferred from Moscow to East Berlin. The agreement stated: 'The documents shall be permanently stored in the central party archive of the Institute of Marxism-Leninism of the Central Committee of the SED.'

After Germany's reunification, the SED's documents were moved to the federal archive. Possibly the first person to access the Reichstag fire files was Hersch Fischler, a private researcher from Düsseldorf. Already in 1992 Fischler had tried to prove that Hans Mommsen had made thirty-three 'errors' in an essay of 1964. He wrote: 'Mistakes occur every time Mommsen gives a factual account that contradicts the account in the original sources, when he confirms Tobias' version even though the original sources contradict Tobias' account, or when Mommsen makes reference to evidence that does not exist in the original sources.' However, most of Fischler's criticism concerned trivial details or were circular arguments. The professor did not react to the accusations, but Reichstag expert Michael S. Cullen worked his way through the article and came to a clear conclusion:

> Fischler wastes his insights by proceeding in a manner that is sectarian, polemic and unscientific. [...] In short, Fischler does little more than Hofer and Calic and their people, who turn circumstantial evidence and hints into irrefutable evidence. They may be in luck when it comes to publishing, but they'll be out of luck with that approach in a German court of law.[76]

However, more than 50,000 pages of original documents constituted a strong argument – Fischler was now at an advantage. In an article in the weekly newspaper *Rheinischer Merkur*, he contested the claim that van der Lubbe had climbed into the Reichstag restaurant. This theory was also championed by Jürgen Schmädeke, who claimed in a popular paperback about the history of the Reichstag that van der Lubbe's various interrogation records contained insoluble contradictions. According to Schmädeke, this suggested that 'van der Lubbe had merely been a tool for the National Socialist arsonists in order to cast suspicion on the communists'. However, an examination of the original files shows that the contradictions Fischler and Schmädeke referred to were insignificant. To the contrary: had van der Lubbe's statements – recorded over a period of several weeks – been even more consistent, then historians would have to ask themselves if they had been engineered. However, for the time being, no such objections were raised as it was inconceivable that the debate surrounding the Reichstag fire would flare up again. Yet this is exactly what happened.[77]

First of all, Alexander Bahar, who had already published the new edition of Hofer's 'Dokumentation', presented a new ally: Wilfried Kugel, a physicist and psychologist, who also had an interest in parapsychology. Kugel seriously suggested that the infamous Berlin clairvoyant Hanussen could have hypnotised van der Lubbe in order to turn him into a tool for the SA arsonists. In 1995, Bahar and Kugel announced supposedly 'newly discovered records' in articles published in the daily newspaper *Neue Zürcher Zeitung* and the academic historical journal *Zeitschrift für Geschichtswissenschaft*. In reality, these were the files that had already been used by Fischler and Schmädeke. Their efforts were again in vain. They tried once more in 1998, on the sixty-fifth anniversary of the arson attack. This time they published a comprehensive dossier in the leftist daily newspaper *taz*. Under the headline 'Historians at Loggerheads Again', the two authors strung together a host of claims that were supposedly supported by the original files in the federal archive, or by the two volumes of the 'Dokumentation' by Hofer. The accusations of forgery were dismissed out of hand, with reference to the report by the Zurich police. Next, the *taz* published another controversial claim: apparently, former 'members of the Nazi coterie, who worked for Rudolf Augstein from 1947', had 'floated' the theory of van der Lubbe as the sole perpetrator. Bahar and Kugel lambasted the *Spiegel* for its 'connection to the Gestapo'. It was true that the magazine had employed a number of journalists who had been closely linked to National Socialism from 1933 to 1945 – but then again, the same could be said for West German society as a whole (and, to a lesser extent, the GDR), even though that is cold comfort. None of these politically compromised journalists had worked on the series about the Reichstag fire, however; it had been overseen by Günther Zacharias, who was born in 1924.[78]

This did not stop Bahar, Kugel and others from repeating their claim, prompted by the decision by Frank Schirrmacher, one of the editors of the *Frankfurter Allgemeine Zeitung*, to award the Ludwig-Börne prize for political journalism to Rudolf Augstein in 2000. First, the award ceremony had to be postponed at short notice because the 77-year-old had fallen ill. Subsequently, a journalist writing for the online publication *Netzeitung* speculated that 'this may not be the true reason for the cancellation'. His key witness was Hersch Fischler, who had accused Augstein of 'personally encouraging the historical misrepresentation of the Reichstag fire'. Fischler argued that the *Spiegel*-founder had helped to 'protect the perpetrators of the genocide of the Jews and to gloss over their crimes'. A few days later, the *Neue Zürcher Zeitung* published an article criticising this alleged 'list of sins' as it could cause 'long-term damage' to Augstein's reputation. These sins supposedly included allocating significant roles within the magazine to former Nazi functionaries, as well as the '*Spiegel* version of the Reichstag fire'. Surprisingly, it was the *Neues Deutschland*, the newspaper of the post-communist *Partei des Demokratischen Sozialismus* [PDS; Party of Democratic Socialism], that came out in support of the conservative Swiss newspaper, believing it was onto 'a first-rate scandal'. *Der Journalist*, the German Federation of Journalists' journal, followed suit shortly after: early in 2001, it described the planned award ceremony as a 'belly flop into murky waters' and the tribute to Augstein as a 'scandal for journalism, a scandal for science'. Hardly anyone took these unfounded and offensive outbursts – so far as they referred to the Reichstag fire – seriously: Rudolf Augstein accepted the well-deserved Börne prize on 13 May 2001. Commenting on the controversy, an article in the *Berliner Morgenpost* read:

> It is right to have a debate about the way in which the *Spiegel's* history should be worked through. It is very unfortunate for this debate to have become associated with the Börne prize. It seems that some colleagues were more interested in knocking an icon of journalism off his pedestal than in reporting the facts. Augstein does not deserve this.[79]

At the same time as attacking the *Spiegel* founder, Bahar, Kugel and Schmädeke made another move. They succeeded in publishing an essay entitled 'The Reichstag Fire: A New Perspective' in the *Historische Zeitschrift*. Essentially, this was based on the files of 1933. The tone of the essay, in keeping with the style of the journal, was relatively neutral and concluded with the statement: 'Further research is possible and necessary.' In the spring of 2000, the newspaper *Die Welt* published several articles about the Reichstag fire, in which all important contributors to the debate were given a chance to have their say. In the end, two opposing camps remained: those who supported the theory of the Nazis having set fire to the Reichstag, and those who took Marinus van der Lubbe and his confessions seriously; there was no progress from a factual point of view. Even though the *Berliner Morgenpost* allocated a generous amount of column space to Bahar and Kugel, as well as Fischler in February 2000, their articles contained nothing new.

The same was true of the 863-page account of the fire that Bahar and Kugel published in 2001. One thing about the incoherently structured volume stood out: it contained, on the inside front cover, a synopsis of the authors' key argument. Entitled 'A Reconstruction of the Reichstag Arson Attack', Bahar and Kugel formulated their view 'subject to all limitations of circumstantial evidence'. They wrote:

> The act must have been planned well before 27 February 1933. The idea appears to have originated from Joseph Goebbels, NSDAP head of propaganda and election co-ordinator for the Reichstag election on 5 March 1933. The aim was to eliminate the KPD and, after pocketing the additional KPD mandates, to secure a (narrow) parliamentary majority for the right-wing parties. Göring offered his assistance, both in his role as president of the Reichstag, as well as making available the Palais, which was connected to the Reichstag building via an underground passageway [...] Some time before the fire, an SA special unit from the Wedding district – presumably with assistance from SA member Adolf Rall, who was later killed by the Gestapo – deposited fire accelerants (phosphor, petroleum, petrol, torches) in the Palais' cellar or in the underground passageway leading to the Reichstag building. On 27 February 1933, at around 8 p.m., a commando consisting of at least three and no more than ten SA men, and led by Hans-Georg Gewehr, arrived in the cellar of the Palais. The men picked up the fire accelerants and entered the Reichstag building via the underground passageway. There, focusing in particular on the plenary chamber, they doused the building, with a self-igniting liquid that was probably only blended on site and which, after a certain latency period, started the fire in the plenary chamber. The commando escaped via the underground passageway [...] At exactly 9 p.m., van der Lubbe was brought

to, and let into, the Reichstag building by the SA. The plenary chamber had already been primed. The sound of breaking glass that was noticed by witnesses, and which was thought to have been caused by van der Lubbe smashing the windows to gain entry, was probably only intended to attract the public's attention. The Dutchman was sacrificed as the only tangible perpetrator and straw man.

This description of the arson attack was impressively concise. However, it contained one important flaw: the authors were unable to prove even one single claim, despite the fact that their book was packed full of references. The original documents did not offer any proof for Bahar and Kugel's theses. Moreover, the synopsis was intrinsically illogical: what would have been the point of drawing the public's attention to the fire by smashing the windows? That would have endangered the alleged arsonists. There had also never been any concrete evidence to suggest the use of a 'self-igniting liquid'. In addition, the underground passageway to the Palais had not been used at the end of February 1933, it had been proven that Hans-Georg Gewehr had no connection to the arson attack, and Adolf Rall had been on remand since 21 December 1932. Despite these shortcomings, the reviews once again ranged from utter praise to scathing criticism. In the *Neue Zürcher Zeitung*, Walther Hofer commended the authors' research; the *Neue Deutschland* newspaper agreed. Hans Mommsen, however, commented: 'The book does not live up to its lofty claims.' Gerhard Hahn, a senior librarian at the *Bundestag*, was also not impressed: 'In a strange way, as a result of their hotchpotch of theses and constructs, the two authors end up questioning their own assumption that the Nazis were the perpetrators, and falsifying those aspects they wished to prove.'[80]

However, none of this stopped editors at the public broadcasting services from investing in productions about the Reichstag fire – productions that featured Brack, Fischler, Bahar and Kugel as authors

131

and key witnesses. First, a film was aired on *Südwestrundfunk* [SWR; Southwest Broadcasting], timed to coincide with the fire's seventieth anniversary. In this forty-four-minute film entitled 'A Fresh Look at the Reichstag Fire', Tina Mendelsohn, with Gerhard Brack as the co-author, attempted to prove that the Nazis were responsible for the arson attack – but without success. The SWR film was nothing more than a reiteration of Fischler's, Hofer's and Schmädeke's claims. The *Frankfurter Allgemeine Zeitung*, which usually took up a neutral position in the debate, reported: 'Unfortunately, Tina Mendelsohn, a bold television journalist, relied too heavily on her sources in this case.' The film ends with the words of one of the trial's witnesses: 'First the Reichstag was on fire, and then the entire world.' Yes, this is true. Yet one must also accept the unpleasant notion that these two events are not connected by a strategic plan, and that sometimes the course of the world is determined by a misguided individual. Once again, when it came to the reviews, exaggerated praise and sharp criticism were to be found side by side: the review in *Die Welt* was scathing, while the *Tagesspiegel* printed a rave review.[81]

Less than three years later, in 2006, Gerhard Brack was again able to persuade a public broadcaster, this time the *Bayrischer Rundfunk* [BR; Bavarian Radio], to commission a lengthy feature programme about the Reichstag fire. For this, the journalists also approached *Spiegel* magazine – although it was not Gerhard Brack who made the enquiry, but a journalist who had previously remained in the background. The magazine's editorial office passed the query on to Klaus Wiegrefe, the historical editor. Wiegrefe initially agreed to give an interview, but hesitated when he realised that Brack was the programme's author. He eventually went ahead with it on the condition that the passages used in the interview would need to be authorised by him first – a perfectly common practice in journalism. When the journalists wanted to change the passages that had already been authorised at short notice,

Wiegrefe was not satisfied with the wording of the new passages and offered to arrange a date for another interview – also a perfectly normal suggestion, as it is not possible to simply make changes to sound clips, as would be the case with printed quotations. When Brack and his colleague declined his offer, Wiegrefe withdrew his interview. Brack then included the following passage in his feature:

> So the *Spiegel* commissions a former Nazi functionary to review the series on the Reichstag fire. To this day, the *Spiegel* struggles to acknowledge that this could be seen as problematic. After discussions that lasted several weeks, Klaus Wiegrefe, the historical editor, finally agreed to an interview. However, ultimately, Wiegrefe did not give us permission to broadcast his interview.

This was a gross distortion of reality by omission – so serious that it was not difficult for the *Spiegel* to first obtain an interim injunction, and then to prevail in two court proceedings: 'The statement the defendant is prohibited from repeating is untrue and violates the claimants' personal rights.' The broadcaster did not lodge an appeal. However, the matter was still not closed: Hersch Fischler complained about the *Spiegel* to the press council, claiming that the magazine had 'demonstrably' published inaccurate information. But this, too, was unfounded: 'The German Press Council takes the view that the German Press Code has not been breached.'[82]

In the debate about the Reichstag fire, Brack and Fischler did not limit their attacks to the *Spiegel*. Since the end of 2000, they had lambasted the Munich *Institut für Zeitgeschichte* in newspaper articles for the events involving Hans Schneider thirty-eight years earlier. The institute's former director, Helmut Krausnick, had had enough when, after more than two years, the essay was still not ready to be published, but merely comprised 330 pages of material 'without being complete'. Krausnick had told Schneider that he was cancelling the assignment and insisted that the author did not use any of the material developed with the institute's help elsewhere. In an internal memorandum about a meeting with the institute's lawyer, employee Hans Mommsen had written:

> As the law stands, the institute is formally unable to withdraw from the contract with Schneider. That is, the institute can reject the publication of the manuscript, but must agree to the publication of the manuscript elsewhere, as long as it does not contain the institute's name or list it as a participant.

Mommsen had continued, apparently paraphrasing the lawyer's statement, that it would be possible to 'put pressure' on Schneider 'to accept a settlement' as 'such a publication would be undesirable for general political reasons'. Schneider had received a small settlement, his manuscript was moved to the institute's archive and Mommsen had written the article about the Reichstag fire.[83]

Decades later, Fischler used Mommsen's memorandum to publish sweeping speculations:

> Helmut Krausnick felt burdened by his NSDAP membership, a fact that was not yet publicly known […]. Is it surprising, then, that the *Institut für Zeitgeschichte* took up the position that it was not possible to refute Tobias' theory about a single perpetrator, and that new findings, like those by Schneider, were not only not published, but suppressed?

At first glance, this seemed like a plausible conclusion. However, when seen in context, the alleged academic scandal did not stand up to scrutiny. Schneider's manuscript, the publication of which had already been announced in the third volume of the Hofer-Calic committee's 'Dokumentation' – supposedly 'ready for print' in 1978, but never published – was indeed nothing more than a poor collection of material full of unproven opinions. Today, readers can see this for themselves, as Fischler published the text as a book in 2004.[84] Krausnick's decision had, therefore, been justified. However, Mommsen in particular had objected to the then institute director's decision not to publish the book, although his further recommendations were indeed unclear. It was, then, not entirely unwarranted that the institute's incumbent management had declared: 'These statements by Hans Mommsen, which have also been quoted by Hersch Fischler, are completely unacceptable from a scientific point of view.' However, Mommsen's memorandum had no effect because Schneider never finalised his manuscript. In any case, this bizarre dispute contributed nothing to the subject in question. Otto Dann, a historian from Cologne, concluded quite rightly that Fischler was solely 'interested in the Schneider "case"' and 'fixated on exposing a "scandal"'. Incidentally, Mommsen himself had explicitly thanked Hans Schneider for 'valuable hints' in an essay from 1964, and noted: 'It remains to be seen whether Schneider will publish his counter-statement, which I am already familiar with from the manuscript.' Had he wanted to suppress its publication, this would have been a foolish thing to do.

Alexander Bahar and Wilfried Kugel's most recent success in their campaign against the theory of Marinus van der Lubbe as the sole perpetrator of the Reichstag fire came in the form of a TV programme on ZDF [*Zweites Deutsches Fernsehen*; Second German Television] in July 2007. As part of its series 'Knowledge: An Adventure', the public service channel broadcast a long report which went to great lengths to illustrate the authors' claims – including fire experiments and the re-enactment of van der Lubbe's route through the Reichstag. However, the ZDF journalists were ill-informed: they claimed that Bahar and Kugel had a 'new hypothesis' when it was in fact already 12 years old, and it apparently did not trouble any of the producers that the actor portraying van der Lubbe had slowly felt his way across the floor plan when in reality he had hurried through the building, as has been proven by several reports following on-site inspections. Once again, Bahar and Kugel were not able to produce any concrete evidence.[85]

10

THE RESOLUTION

THE DEBATE – A SUMMARY

The debate about 27 February 1933 has been going on for three-quarters of a century. During this time, dozens of books that focus entirely or predominantly on the Reichstag fire and the subsequent trials have been published, as well as more than 100 academic essays and thousands of newspaper articles. The files documenting the preliminary enquiry and the trial at the Supreme Court comprise exactly 50,494 pages. These can easily be accessed by anyone who is interested at the federal archive in Berlin. And yet, the situation remains as unclear as it was immediately after the event when, on the one hand, Wolfgang Stresemann and Harry Graf Kessler automatically assumed that the Nazis were responsible for the arson attack, and, on the other hand, the investigating police officers Helmut Heisig and Walter Zirpins were already convinced that van der Lubbe was telling the truth: 'The question whether van der Lubbe carried this act out alone can be confirmed without hesitation.'

Despite repeated claims, nobody has been able to produce evidence to prove that members of the NSDAP carried out the arson attack. Apart from rumours, biased testimonies and dubious expert reports, as well as a number of badly forged 'documents', nothing to suggest that the Nazis are guilty has emerged in the past seventy-five years. Yet despite this (or even in full awareness of the fact that there is no such evidence), people speculate about the wildest imaginable conspiracies. In 1987, this led Peter Haungs, a political scientist, to pose the incredulous question: 'What is the matter with German historians? Or: is the falsification of sources a trivial offence?' It is unlikely that new, genuine evidence will be uncovered now; no important sources are still missing. Anyone who in 1933 could have found out something hitherto unknown, and who could have broken their silence, is long-since dead. As, on the whole, nothing new has emerged in the past few years – and probably will not in the future – supporters of the conspiracy theories have begun to focus their attention on other things. These include, for example, launching savage attacks on Rudolf Augstein, who is, in the best sense, the perhaps most influential journalist in West Germany, or on the *Institut für Zeitgeschichte*, which has contributed to an unbiased working-through of the Nazi past as few other institutions have done. And thus defamation has replaced methodically sound historiography.[86]

In contrast, the account of the arson attack by Marinus van der Lubbe is coherent and convincing. According to the Dutch anarcho-communist, he had wanted to take a stand against the Nazis' seizure of power and against the hamstrung radical workers' movement with his act; it was to represent a revolution from below, or even upheaval as an end in itself. Over the course of more than thirty interrogations that took place over several months, van der Lubbe essentially repeated the same account – the relevant files do not contain any significant contradictions. Having confessed his guilt, van der Lubbe even went on hunger strike to bring an end to the seemingly never-ending interrogations. However, he did not succeed; he continued to be questioned. It also did not seem to trouble the investigating judge and the prosecutor that all the objective pieces of evidence collected in the Reichstag between the end of February and the beginning of March 1933 supported van der Lubbe's account, or at least did not contradict it. For instance, crime scene investigations by Commissar Walter Bunge, a fire expert, found, among other things, 'definite evidence of fingerprints' at the point of entry identified by van der Lubbe. However, they could not be identified because the surface was so rough. On the other hand, the files of the preliminary investigation contain no indication that several offenders had been involved and their traces hushed up or forged. Indeed, this would have been strange, as the Nazis would have had no interest in suppressing evidence that suggested further accomplices – they maintained, after all, that van der Lubbe had not acted alone. Yet although the police were clearly put under pressure to 'find' evidence, nothing was found to suggest additional offenders, any sort of fire accelerant or an ignition system that the 'vagabond' van der Lubbe would not have had access to. The list detailing the 'seized pieces of evidence' from the Reichstag had ninety-nine entries, yet not a single one of them pointed to anything other than the arsonist's description of the arson attack. This did not stop several experts from coming up with wild speculations in order to meet their clients' wishes. However, their expert reports simply could not withstand impartial scrutiny.[87]

Moreover, had the arson attack indeed been the result of a perfidious plan by the SA or the NSDAP, then the obviously unscrupulous perpetrators surely would have been clever enough to leave sufficient 'traces' to make sure their plan succeeded. If one considers the real Nazi provocation six and a half years later – the staged attack on 31 August 1939, when SS men posing as Poles attacked the German radio station *Sender Gleiwitz* – it is clear that the use of false evidence was not alien to Hitler's henchmen. To not think the Nazis capable of being so calculating in 1933 would mean to greatly underestimate them. In addition, if they really had been responsible for the Reichstag fire, surely they could have manipulated the rules of procedure in the Supreme Court in such a way that a criminal division – suitably brought into line – would have passed the desired sentence. Instead, not only the three Bulgarian defendants were acquitted, but the German communist Torgler was, too. The German government became an international laughing stock. Joseph Goebbels made a note of a conversation with Hitler in his diary on 9 April 1941: 'He thinks Torgler is guilty of Reichstag fire. Out of the question. He's much too bourgeois for that.' However, the 'Führer' held on to his belief. On 29 December 1941, he told his closest confidantes during one of his night-time monologues: 'I am convinced that Torgler set the Reichstag on fire, but I can't prove it.' Why would the dictator deliberately have lied to his confidantes, about the Reichstag fire of all things, when he was usually so outspoken in their company?[88]

Conspiracy theory versus circumstantial evidence: when faced with such a point of departure, historians and journalists would usually not hesitate to pass judgement. However, when it comes to the Reichstag fire, the same does not hold true. Why has the dispute about the perpetrators not been resolved? The most important reason is probably the fact that, given the Nazis' numerous and far worse crimes, it is easy to believe that they committed the arson attack as well. Those capable of plunging the whole world into war and killing millions of people would certainly not have shied away from starting a fire. Second, Hitler and Göring really did expertly exploit the fire for their purposes: the deliberately showcased explosion of force within domestic politics in March 1933 marked the beginning of the total seizure of power in Germany. However, the fact that the NSDAP and the SA benefited from the crime does not prove that they also committed it. A third reason is the Supreme Court's conclusion that van der Lubbe must have had accomplices. After acquitting the four communist co-defendants due to lack of evidence, this was probably the judges' concession to the government, that is, an attempt to appease those now in power.

There is overwhelming evidence to suggest that Marinus van der Lubbe's confession should be taken seriously. So why, for the past seventy-five years, has the question regarding the perpetrator(s) been so incredibly controversial? Why, of all things, does this arson attack have the potential to cause such tremendous agitation? Why is it so important for contemporary German history? After all, the fact that the Nazis were innocent just this once does not lessen the horror of the Holocaust or of the war of extermination perpetrated by the SS and the *Wehrmacht*. The answer lies in the fundamental view of the Third Reich: was the arson attack part of the NSDAP's carefully prepared plan? Or did the 'Führer' and his paladins react to the Reichstag fire spontaneously; was it their ruthlessness that prevailed against the hesitant political opponents – social democracy and the *Zentrum*? Whoever believes that the Reichstag fire was a stunt, must inevitably define the Nazi dictatorship overall as a rigorously planned *Machtpolitik* [power politics] – including Auschwitz. This assumption, however, has one inescapable implication: the responsibility of German society as a whole, of hundreds of thousands, even millions of Germans, for all those crimes is automatically very much reduced. If, namely, the seizure of power in 1933 had indeed been the result of a careful plan, with the Reichstag fire at its heart, then that would turn the majority of Germans into victims of a meticulous plan that was ruthlessly executed. Thus, the assumption that the Nazis are guilty ultimately exculpates German society at that time. Those who believe in this fictitious version of events are holding onto the state of research of the 1950s; that of the past century.

Those, on the other hand, who support the notion that van der Lubbe indeed acted alone, see the systematic criminal activity during the Third Reich as a result of National Socialist ideology and the ressentiments of countless Germans, as well as coincidence. From this perspective, the murder of millions of European Jews presents as a gradual process at the initiative of regional commanders, a 'cumulative radicalisation' that culminated in the German murder factories in Poland. Of course, Hitler's thinking contained constants, such as the dream of conquering *Lebensraum* ['living space'] to the East, and his racial fanaticism, which led to mass murder. However, without broad support from society, the 'Führer and Reich chancellor' would never have been able to realise his hate-filled ideas. It is altogether too simplistic to assume that Hitler took Germany by surprise and then ensured his continued rule by means of tyranny. In reality, the relationship between the regime and society was much more complex – a view that has been unanimously confirmed by recent scholarship about the Third Reich. Until well into the Second World War, the Third Reich was a popular dictatorship. Hitler's aggressive politics – domestic and foreign – did not, it appears, contradict the wishes of large parts of the population, however painful this may be in retrospect.

One last question remains: what caused the devastating fire in the plenary chamber if Marinus van der Lubbe, along with his – at first seemingly inadequate – resources such as firelighters, items of clothing and tablecloths, really was the perpetrator? After all, four out of the five fire experts questioned at the time ruled out the possibility of a single arsonist sparking such a firestorm – even if one of the four experts was honest enough to admit that it was a mystery, while the other three preferred to speculate. It is of course impossible to prove anything conclusively seventy-five years after the event. Although exhibits would certainly have been stored, they did not survive the Second World War. There is thus no starting point for a modern investigation with vastly superior scientific methods than those used in 1933. A re-enactment of the fire is unsuitable, precisely because it has not been possible to reconstruct in detail the exact circumstances of that cold Monday night. Nonetheless, recent advances in the field of fire science can offer clues as to what most likely happened in the plenary chamber. What needs to be explained is how it was possible for the enormous conference room to catch fire so suddenly, when van der Lubbe had focused on setting aflame the heavy curtains near the president's table and at the chamber's western exit on the opposite side, as he had repeatedly stated during the interrogations. Was it caused by some sort of incendiary materials that had been spread around the plenary chamber and that were somehow sparked off? In this case it really would have had to be a conspiracy, with the young Dutchman as a tool or scapegoat.

If, however, the statements of the firefighters who were at the scene at the time are read in view of the latest findings in modern fire science, then the mystery is easily solved. What happened on 27 February 1933 at around 9.27 p.m. was most likely what is today known as a 'backdraft' – a dangerous phenomenon that can occur during fires in enclosed spaces. In such cases, an openly burning fire at first uses up most of the available oxygen. Once the flames go out, the significantly elevated temperature causes a chemical reaction called pyrolysis. When this happens, organic molecules break down, and unoxidised, combustible gases rise and collect under the ceiling. At the same time, the temperature drops slightly as the fire reduces to smouldering. This creates a vacuum that pulls in air as soon as this is possible. If oxygen then enters the room, a catastrophe is almost inevitable. When a door is opened, the pent-up heat first appears to rush out, only to be immediately pulled back in by a sharp draft. Now the oxygen mixes with the hot gases – depending on the size of the room, this sometimes only takes a few seconds, but can take up to more than one minute. As soon as the mixture becomes ignitable, a flue gas explosion occurs, which generates temperatures as high as 1,000°C, and which can no longer be brought under control.

143

All known details of the fire in the plenary chamber correspond to the 'backdraft' phenomenon. Marinus van der Lubbe set fire to the panels of fabric on both sides of the president's table and next to the stenographer's desk. These would have been dusty and therefore would have burned very well. As has been verified, the ventilation in the plenary chamber had been turned off, and for at least a few minutes none of the doors had been opened. It must have been the president's desk and the benches at the front, which had been cleaned with detergents and treated with wax for decades, that released the combustible gases that collected under the air-tight glass ceiling. As there was no longer sufficient oxygen to keep the open fire going, the temperature dropped slightly, creating a vacuum. The testimonies confirm this description: Maintenance Manager Alexander Scranowitz and Police Lieutenant Emil Lateit both saw open flames. A few minutes later, Fire Chief Waldemar Klotz noticed lots of smoke, but no open flames; he also felt the pressure coming from the pent-up, high temperature. Based on his experience, he closed the swing door to the plenary chamber as quickly as he could in order to prevent 'darting flames'. Klotz told his men to get a hose in order to cool down the plenary chamber. Senior Fire Chief Emil Puhle recalled the way the draft had pulled back; his colleague Willi König remembered its force. All firefighters who had been at the scene reported, in different words, how awed they had been by the force of the explosive combustion and the sea of flames that followed. However, as the 'backdraft' phenomenon had not yet been discovered, they were merely able to give an account of their impressions, rather than systematically describe it.[89]

And so the last remaining mystery surrounding the Reichstag fire is solved, without having to resort to conspiracy theories. It was Police Lieutenant Lateit, Maintenance Manager Scranowitz and the firefighters themselves who caused the fire to spread so explosively by opening the doors to the plenary chamber. The complex chemical phenomenon was the only igniter that was needed. Instinctively, the fire experts could perhaps have known better, yet one can only speculate whether the destruction of the plenary chamber could have been avoided. 'First the Reichstag was on fire, and then the entire world.' This statement is correct. However, those who were responsible for the second, much worse catastrophe, were not identical with the arsonist who caused the first fire. Thus, seventy-five years of controversy end with one simple truth: Marinus van der Lubbe acted alone.

NOTES

CHAPTER 1

1   For the weather, see *Berliner Morgenpost*, 26 February 1933;
    for the general situation that day, see *Berliner Tageblatt* and
    Vossische Zeitung, 27 February 1933 (evening editions); for more
    information on the events following Hitler's appointment, see
    Bracher/Sauer/Schulz: *Die nationalsozialistische Machtergreifung*,
    pp.31–74, and Kellerhoff: *Hitlers Berlin*, pp.91–4, as well as
    Friedrich: *Missbrauchte Hauptstadt*, pp.422–32.
2   For information on the Reichstag that day, see Scranowitz
    statement: BA Berlin R 3003/2, Bl.44; for the occupancy of
    KPD-headquarters, see *Berliner Morgenpost*, 24 February 1933,
    and *Berliner Lokalanzeiger*, 28 February 1933 (evening edition);
    for the SPD event, see *Vorwärts*, 28 February 1933 (morning
    edition), and Sandvoß: *Die 'andere' Reichshauptstadt*, p.55f, as well
    as *Berliner Tageblatt*, 28 February 1933 (morning edition); for the
    preparations by the police, see Lateit statement: BA Berlin R
    3003/53, Bl.112–14.

3   For Flöter's role, see Flöter statement: BA Berlin R 3003/109,
    Bl.21; for the reduced street lamp capacity, see letter by Gasag:
    BA Berlin R 3003/54, Bl.80; for Flöter's conduct, see *Spiegel*,
    21 October 1959. All subsequent time specifications are based
    on a critical comparison of recorded estimates (especially report
    by Wagner: BA Berlin R 43 II/294, Bl.111-13 and report by
    fire investigation unit: BA Berlin R 3003/53, Bl.62) and Berndt:
    Zur Entstehung, pp.77–90, as well as Fischler: *Zum Zeitablauf*,
    pp.620–32. It is not possible to reconstruct the sequence of
    events to the minute and with absolute certainty. This is due
    in part to the fact that only mechanical clocks existed in 1933,
    and partly because the times given by various people were
    based on their own watch, or were only estimates, as several of
    those questioned conceded in the minutes. However, the times
    given in the book, which in some instances correct those of
    eyewitnesses by a few minutes, are likely to correspond to the
    true course of events.

4   See Buwert statement: BA Berlin, R 3003/1, Bl. 6f. and
    R 3003/2, Bl. 51f., as well as R 3003/53, Bl. 151f.; for Thaler's
    impressions, see Thaler statement: BA Berlin, R 3003/1, Bl.
    17f. and R 3003/53, Bl. 181–6r; 'Run', Buwert cited in Tobias:
    Reichstagsbrand, p.15; for the alarm at the 'Haus der Ingenieure',
    see Wally Freudenberg statement: BA Berlin R 3003/1, Bl. 19
    and R 3003/2, Bl. 195f., also see Emil Lück statement: BA
    Berlin R 3003/54, Bl. 24–6, as well as Hermann Freudenberg
    statement: BA Berlin R 3003/53, Bl. 72; for the emergency
    call to the fire brigade, see Schaeske statement: BA Berlin
    R 3003/1, Bl. 129, as well as Kurz statement: BA Berlin R
    3003/2, Bl. 191f.

5   'Carefully enough', Gempp (ed.): *Berliner Feuerwehr –
    Dienstanweisung*, p.12; for Police Lieutenant Emil Lateit's

course of action, see Lateit statement: BA Berlin R 3003/53, Bl. 112–25 (he changed his statement during a later interview and said that he had not noticed the unusual heat when he looked into the plenary chamber): BA Berlin R 3003/55, Bl. 175); for the entry into the incident book, see Lateit statement: BA Berlin R 3003/1, Bl. 8f.; for Wendt, see Losigkeit statement: BA Berlin R 3003/53, Bl. 126f.; for Wendt and the following, see Scranowitz statement: BA Berlin R 3003/2, Bl. 44–9, as well as his anonymous eyewitness report in the *Vossische Zeitung*, 28 February 1933 (evening edition).

6   For the operation by Linienstraße fire station, see Puhle statement: BA Berlin R 3003/2, Bl. 41–3, as well as R 3003/53, Bl. 14f.; Puhle statement: BA Berlin R 3003/2, Bl. 43r. and, with the same title, *Berliner Tageblatt* of 28 February 1933 (morning edition); 'darting flames', Klotz statement: BA Berlin R 3003/2, Bl. 36r.

7   'Suddenly', report by Wagner: BA Berlin R 43 II/294, Bl. 125; 'up towards', Puhle statement: BA Berlin R 3003/53, Bl. 14f.; 'I could see', Klotz statement: BA Berlin R 3003/2, Bl. 36f.; 'never experienced', Polchow statement: BA Berlin R 3003/53, Bl. 16; 'flames of a forge', König statement: BA Berlin R 3003/53, Bl. 60; 'audible pop', verdict by RG [*Reichsgericht*; Supreme Court of the German Reich], 23 December 1933 (collection Kellerhoff), p.26; 'a rocket had exploded', *Berliner Lokalanzeiger*, 28 February 1933 (morning edition).

8   For Scranowitz's and Poeschel's route, see Scranowitz statement: BA Berlin R 3003/2, Bl. 44–9 and Poeschel statement: BA Berlin R 3003/1, Bl.11f. and R 3003/53, Bl. 68; see verdict by RG, 23 December 1933 (collection Kellerhoff), p.24f.; for van der Lubbe's arrival at the police station, see Lateit statement: BA Berlin, R 3003/53, Bl. 20–2 and Poeschel statement:

BA Berlin R 3003/53, Bl. 68 (time stated: 9.40 p.m. until
9.45 p.m.).

CHAPTER 2

9   For the alarms, see records by fire investigation unit: BA Berlin
R 3003/53, Bl. 62; for communication within the fire services,
see Leske: 'Notruf der Feuerwehr', p.69; for the fire brigade's
response procedure, see Gempp (ed.): *Berliner Feuerwehr –
Dienstanweisung*, pp.15–17; for Gempp, see *Völkischer Beobachter*,
15/16 October 1933; 'difficult job', *Berliner Morgenpost*,
28 February 1933.

10   'Surrounded by', and 'sparks are flying', *Berliner Tageblatt*,
28 February 1933 (morning edition).

11   'At this point', reader letter Thielitz: *Welt*, 15 March 2000;
'many others' and 'control the crowds', *Vossische Zeitung*,
28 February 1933 (morning edition); 'several thousand',
Berliner Tageblatt, 28 February 1933 (morning edition); for the
time period after the area had been cordoned-off, see Bahar/
Kugel: *Reichstagsbrand*, p.126; 'Enormous flames', *Berliner
Lokalanzeiger*, 28 Feburary 1933 (morning edition); 'On all
sides', *Berliner Morgenpost*, 28 February 1933; for fire suppression
tactics, see ibid. and also Gempp, cited in *Völkischer Beobachter*,
3 March 1933; for the danger facing the entire building, see
Berliner Morgenpost, 28 February 1933 and *Berliner Lokalanzeiger*,
28 February 1933 (morning edition).

12   'The glass cupola', François-Poncet: *Botschafter*, p.106f.

13   'Hitler's hotel costs' and 'Sir', Hanfstaengl: *Zwischen Weißem und
Braunem Haus*, pp.291–5; 'Hitler and Auwi', Goebbels: *Tagebücher*,
part I, vol. 2/III, p.137 (28 February 1933); in the version edited

for publication in 1934, the same passage of the diary reads as follows: 'The Führer comes for dinner at 9 p.m. We make music and chat. Suddenly, a phone call from Dr Hanfstaengl: "The Reichstag is on fire!" I think he is imagining things and refuse to inform the Führer. I ask around and then receive the terrible confirmation: it is true. The building is ablaze, with flames darting out of the cupola. Arson! I inform the Führer straight away and then we race down the Charlottenburger Chaussee towards the Reichstag at 100 kilometres an hour.' Goebbels: *Vom Kaiserhof*, p.269f.

14   'Muck out', *Völkischer Beobachter*, 16 February 1933; 'I expect', circular by the Reich commissar for the Prussian Ministry of the Interior, 17 February 1933, quoted in Becker (ed.): *Hitlers Machtergreifung*, p.75; for the reports made to Göring, see Adermann statement: BA Berlin R 3003/46, Bl. 29r, as well as Scranowitz statement: BA Berlin R 3003/2, Bl. 44r; 'This is', Göring, quoted in report from Grauert, in Tobias: *Reichstagsbrand*, p.109; the speculation that Göring had already entered the Reichstag at 9.19 p.m. is untenable – it is based on a biased interpretation of eyewitness reports, as well as unreliable press sources; examples of this can be found in Bahar/Kugel: *Reichstagsbrand*, pp.127–37; 'I ran across' and 'The press', Reed: *Burning of Reichstag*, p.16f.

15   'Around a quarter', Gempp, quoted in *Völkischer Beobachter*, 15/16 October 1933; 'The fire-fighting operations', *Berliner Tageblatt*, 28 February 1933 (morning edition); 'Don't mind me', Gempp, quoted in *Völkischer Beobachter* 15/16 October 1933.

16   'The entire building', Goebbels: *Tagebücher*, part I, vol. 2/III, p.137 (28 Feburary 1933); 'Oh God', Delmer: *Die Deutschen und ich*, p.187; 'The Reichstag', 'There is no doubt', 'Here you can see' and 'This is a', *Daily Express*, 28 February 1933, quoted

in Bahar/Kugel: *Der Reichstagsbrand*, p.159; see Sefton Delmer's report twenty-six years later: *Spiegel*, 25 November 1959 and, with some deviating details, Delmer: *Die Deutschen und ich*, pp.187–203; 'This is' and 'There will be', Diels: *Lucifer ante portas*, p.193; 'fight against', Weiß (ed.): *Biographisches Lexikon*, p.84; 'This is', Diels: *Lucifer ante portas*, p.194.

17 'Minister Göring', Wilhelm Schneider (i.e. Heinrich Schnitzler), quoted in Tobias: *Der Reichstagsbrand*, p.9; 10.30 p.m., see record of admission: BA Berlin R 3003/1, Bl. 15.

18 'By half past ten', *Berliner Morgenpost*, 28 February 1933; 'Now, around half past ten', 'Even now' and 'fire's force', *Berliner Tageblatt*, 28 February 1933 (morning edition); 'Shortly after 11 p.m.' and 'the fire started', *Vossische Zeitung*, 28 February 1933 (morning edition); for the situation around midnight, see the almost identical articles in *Vossische Zeitung*, *Berliner Lokalanzeiger* and *Berliner Tageblatt*, 28 February 1933 (all morning editions); fire under control, see telegram by police headquarters, 27 February 1933, 11.57 p.m.: BA Berlin R 3003/1, Bl. 4; 'dampening down', *Berliner Tageblatt*, 28 February 1933 (morning edition).

CHAPTER 3

19 'I have been', see interrogation of van der Lubbe, 2 March 1933: BA Berlin R 3003/1, Bl. 63; 'He denied', Bonhoeffer/ Zutt: Über den Geisteszustand, p.675, and their original report: BA Berlin R 3003/3, Bl. 58–62.

20 For his biography, see interrogation of van der Lubbe about personal details, 28 February 1933: BA Berlin R 3003/1, Bl. 58f., report by Leiden police (translation), 2 March 1933:

BA Berlin R 3003/53, Bl. 214–18 and indictment: BA Berlin
R 3003/10, Bl. 10–13r, also Karasek: *Der Brandstifter*, pp.11–29,
35–43, as well as Soer (ed.): *Marinus van der Lubbe*, passim, and
Schouten: *Marinus van der Lubbe*, pp.15–59; 'Aged 19', ibid., p.21;
'Those unemployed', cited in ibid., p.49.

21 'In the Netherlands' and 'I have noticed', see interrogation of
van der Lubbe, 2 March 1933: BA Berlin R 3003/1, Bl. 63f.;
'root and branch', cited in Becker (ed.): *Hitlers Machtergreifung*,
p.40; 'I have realised', see interrogation of van der Lubbe,
2 March 1933: BA Berlin R 3003/1, Bl. 63–4r.

22 'I can', see statement by van der Lubbe, 30 March 1933:
BA Berlin R 3003/4, Bl. 63; confirmation by sales assistants:
BA Berlin R 3003/1, Bl. 49f.; for the sequence of events of the
first arson attack, see ibid. R 3003/1, Bl. 59 and van der Lubbe's
own sketch of the arson attack: BA Berlin R 3003/1, Bl. 55, as
well as verdict by RG, 23 December 1933, p.13f.; photographs
of the crime scene taken by the fire investigation unit confirm
van der Lubbe's description in detail, see BA Berlin R 3003/225.

23 'Building representing', interrogation of van der Lubbe, 2 March
1933: BA Berlin R 3003/1, Bl. 63f.; 'I saw that', interrogation of
van der Lubbe, 28 February 1933: BA Berlin R 3003/1, Bl. 59f.
(the former Rathausstraße is now called Gustav-Böß-Straße);
'flammable substances', Kiekbusch statement: BA Berlin R
3003/56, Bl. 69f.; see van der Lubbe's sketch of the arson attack:
BA Berlin R 3003/1, Bl. 56; photographs of the crime scene
taken by the fire investigation unit confirm van der Lubbe's
description in detail, see BA Berlin R 3003/226.

24 'It was situated', interrogation of van der Lubbe, 2 March
1933: BA Berlin R 3003/1, Bl. 63f.; 'I crossed' and 'I threw',
interrogation of van der Lubbe, 28 February 1933: BA Berlin
R 3003/1, Bl. 59f.; see van der Lubbe's sketch of the arson attack:

BA Berlin R 3003/1, Bl. 56; for the fast response to the fire in the palace, see statement by in-house fire service: BA Berlin R 3003/63, Bl. 63–8; photographs of the crime scene taken by the fire investigation unit confirm van der Lubbe's description, see BA Berlin R 3003/227; see for example coverage by *Berliner Lokalanzeiger* and *Berliner Tageblatt*, 27 February 1933 (evening editions), as well as *Berliner Morgenpost*, 28 February 1933.

25 'System's central point', interrogation of van der Lubbe, 2 March 1933: R 3003/1, Bl. 63f.; 'awful appearance', verdict by RG, 23 December 1933, p.16; 'like a tramp', Schmal statement: BA Berlin R 3003/3, Bl. 20; 'I chose' and 'with around ten kicks', interrogation of van der Lubbe, 1 March 1933: BA Berlin R 3003/1, Bl. 61f.; for the nearest street lamp, see blueprint of Gasag plan: BA Berlin R 3003/54, Bl. 84.

26 'Through the flames', interrogation of van der Lubbe, 1 March 1933: BA Berlin R 3003/1, Bl. 61f., as well as 29 March 1933: BA Berlin R 3003/4, Bl. 61; for the review by the investigators, see report by fire investigation unit: BA Berlin R 3003/6, Bl. 52f. and *Berliner Morgenpost*, 22 October 1933, for the on-site inspection the previous day.

27 'The question' and 'Van der Lubbe gave', final report Zirpins: BA Berlin R 3003/1, Bl. 73; ibid. the question mark in blue.

CHAPTER 4

28 For the time period of the night-time meeting at the interior ministry, see *Vossische Zeitung*, 28 February 1933 (morning edition); 'seemingly never-ending', Heinrich Schnitzler, cited in Mommsen: *Der Reichstagsbrand*, p.385; see Diels: *Lucifer*, p.193f.; 'Hitler is enraged', Goebbels: *Tagebücher*, part I, vol. 2 III,

p.137 (28 February 1933); see the doctored description in
the published version of his 'Tagebuchblätter' [diary pages] in
1934: 'The Führer stays calm throughout; it is admirable to see
him giving orders, the same man who was casually chatting
at our dining table just half an hour ago.' Goebbels: *Vom
Kaiserhof*, p.270.

29   'Decree for the Protection of the German People', 4 February
1933 in: *Reichsgesetzblatt* [Reich Law Gazette] I 1933,
pp.35–40; 'Decree against Treason and Treasonous Activities',
28 February 1933, in: *Reichsgesetzblatt* I 1933, p.86f.; 'Decree
for the Protection of People and State', 28 February 1933,
Reichsgesetzblatt I 1933, p.83.

30   For the first wave of arrests, see *Berliner Tageblatt* and *Vossische
Zeitung*, 28 February 1933 (evening editions); for the legal basis
for the arrest warrants, see as example the arrest warrant for
Egon Erwin Kirsch, as facsimile: www.Netzeitung.de/servlets/
page?section=685&item=127912.html (last viewed 15 February
2007); for the further arrests in Berlin, as well as those in
Hanover, see *Berliner Tageblatt*, 1 March 1933 (morning edition);
for the arrests in Cologne, see *Berliner Tageblatt*, 2 March 1933
(morning edition).

31   For Hitler's and Goebbels' activities in the early hours of
28 February, see Goebbels: *Tagebücher*, part I, vol. 2/III,
p.137 (28 February 1933), as well as, for the most part similar,
Goebbels: *Vom Kaiserhof*, p.270f.; also *Angriff*, 28 February
1933; 'Basic Law of the Third Reich', Krausnick, in:
Eschenburg et al.: *Der Weg in die Diktatur*, p.183; for the
re-evaluation of the Reichstag Fire Decree, see Raithel/
Strenge: *Die Reichstagsbrandverordnung*, pp.413–60; if there ever
was a 'Basic Law of the Third Reich' (the Weimar constitution
officially remained in effect until 1945), then it was the Enabling
Act of 24 March 1933.

32 'The chancellor', 'poison as a means', 'a single perpetrator',
    'the detainee' and 'Today', see minutes of ministers' meeting,
    28 February 1933, 11.00 a.m.: BA Berlin R 43 I/1459, Bl.
    755–60; Göring had apparently received a carbon copy of the first
    interrogation records before the meeting: BA Berlin R 3003/1, Bl.
    58–60r and R 3003/5, Bl. 46–53.

33 'I have been told' and 'to make use of', Göring to Daluege,
    28 February 1933: BA Berlin R 43 II/1193, Bl. 41; 'We have
    learned that', *Berliner Tageblatt*, 28 February 1933 (evening
    edition); 'fifteen tons of explosives', Meissner: *Ebert, Hindenburg,
    Hitler*, p.273f.

34 For the 'wild concentration camps', see Benz/Distel: *Ort des
    Terrors*, pp.39–65; Bräutigam/Gliech: *Zwangslager*, pp.141–72;
    for Friedrichstraße 234, see ibid. p.157; 7,784 people in
    'protective custody', see Broszat: *Nationalsozialistische
    Konzentrationslager*, p.20.

35 For information on *Sturmlokal* Drechsel, see Bräutigam/
    Gliech: *Zwangslager*, p.160; 'The permitted', Göring circular
    decree, 3 March 1933, cited in Broszat: *Nationalsozialistische
    Konzentrationslager*, p.15; 'loyalty and discipline', Röhm appeal,
    4 March 1933, cited in Longerich: *Braune Bataillone*, p.166f.; Wolff
    report in: *Prozess gegen die Hauptkriegsverbrecher*, vol. 28, pp.242–4.

36 'He did not doubt', minutes of ministers' meeting, 28 February
    1933, 11.00 a.m.: BA Berlin R 43 I/1459, Bl. 755; Law to
    Remedy the Distress of People and Reich, 24 March 1933, in:
    Reichsgesetzblatt I 1933, p.141.

37 'To hang the culprit', minutes of ministers' meeting, 2 March
    1933, 12.00 p.m.: BA Berlin R 43 I/1460, Bl. 5; 'imperative'
    and 'Even though', see minutes of ministers' meeting, 7 March
    1933, 4.15 p.m.: BA Berlin R 43 I/1460, Bl. 30f.; report,
    4 March 1933: BA Berlin R 43 II/294, Bl. 27–36; for the

counter-opinion, see files of the Reich Chancellery, Hitler government, vol. 1, p.217f., ref. 22; Schlegelberger became an enforcer of National Socialist legal policy and was sentenced to life imprisonment in 1947; 'apparently intended', 'did most certainly' and 'lawfully in every way', record by Neurath: BA Berlin R 43 II/294, Bl. 85–93.

CHAPTER 5

38 'I hope', Rosenberg, cited in Delmer, *Spiegel*, 25 November 1959, as well as, slightly differently, in Delmer: *Die Deutschen und ich*, p.188; for information on the way rumours develop, see Keil/Kellerhoff: *Gerüchte machen Geschichte*, pp.9–26.

39 'People were running', Buwert statement: BA Berlin R 3003/1, Bl. 6f; 'prevent the culprits', Lateit statement: BA Berlin R 3003/1, Bl. 8f.; 'Looking at the fire', Poeschel statement: BA Berlin R 3003/1, Bl. 11f.; 'piles of cleaning rags', *Berliner Morgenpost*, 28 February 1933; for the suggestion that it might have been van der Lubbe on his own, see *Vossische Zeitung*, 28 February 1933 (evening edition).

40 'The midnight news', 'We were shocked' and 'My father', Ebermayer: *Denn heute gehört uns Deutschland*, p.31f.; 'My phone', Stresemann: *Wie konnte es geschehen?*, p.66; 'Nobody I have spoken to', Kessler: *Tagebücher*, p.703f.; 'Several details' and 'The possibility', François-Poncet report, 28 February 1933, cited in Becker (ed.): *Hitlers Machtergreifung*, p.104f.

41 'The official communiqué', *Le Temps*, 1 March 1933, cited in *Braunbuch* I, p.73; 'No sensible', *Daily Telegraph*, 3 March 1933, cited in *Braunbuch* I, p.74; 'German capitalists', *Iswestia*, 2 March 1933, cited in *Los Angeles Times*, 3 March 1933; *Chicago Daily*

Tribune, 5 March 1933; 'it ought to be checked', minutes of ministers' meeting, 2 March 1933, 12.00 p.m.: BA Berlin R 43 I/1460, Bl. 4f.

42 For the fabrications about Torgler, see *Völkischer Beobachter*, 1 and 2 March 1933, as well as *Angriff*, 1 March 1933; 'In response to', Torgler statement: BA Berlin R 3003/1, Bl. 30f.; 'Hired arsonists', flyer of KPD Saxony, 28 February 1933 (collection Kellerhoff); 'Reichstag fire provocation', appeal by the KPD central committee, 1 March 1933, cited in *Reichstagsbrandprozess*, vol. 1, p.53f.; 'The arson attack', *Rundschau über Politik, Wirtschaft und Arbeiterbewegung*, 1 March 1933, cited in *Reichstagsbrandprozess*, vol. 1, p.58; 'the fascists', *Prawda*, 1 March 1933, cited in *Reichstagsbrandprozess*, vol. 1, p.63.

43 'Elimination of Marxism', *Völkischer Beobachter*, 2 March 1933; 'I'm listening', Goebbels: *Tagebücher*, part I, vol. 2/III, p.139 (3 March 1933); 'secret plans', *Völkischer Beobachter*, 3 March 1933; 'any information', appeal by chief constable of Berlin, 3 March 1933 (collection Kellerhoff); for Sörnewitz and Weinberg, see the records of the fire investigation unit: BA Berlin R 3003/4, Bl. 1–83, 100–25; for the arrest of Dimitroff and the other two Bulgarians, see the investigation file: BA Berlin R 3003/35.

44 'On the recommendation', appeal by KPD central committee, no date, cited in Becker (ed.): *Hitlers Machtergreifung*, p.126; for Wessel, see Kellerhoff: *Ortstermin Mitte*, pp.144–51.

45 For Münzenberg's time in Paris, see Groß: *Münzenberg*, pp.246–56 and McMeekin: *The red millionaire*, pp.255–65; 'effeminate', 'in every fibre' and 'love list', *Braunbuch*, p.52, 56f.; 'pathological liar', ibid., illustration before p.153.

46 'Meanwhile', memorandum cited in: *Wer hat den Reichstag angezündet?*, p.6f.; for the date of 18 April 1933, see

Reichstagsbrandprozess, vol. 1, p.212, ref. 2; 'diplomatic storm', *New York Times*, 28 April 1933; 'A supposed special correspondent' and 'arsonists are members', *Völkischer Beobachter*, 28 April 1933; 'accusation like this' and 'condemn such publications', Telegraphen-Union, cited in *New York Times*, 28 April 1933; copies of *Manchester Guardian* article as leaflets, for example in: BA Berlin R 3003/8, Bl. 73 (envelope).

47   For Oberfohren's suicide, see *New York Times*, 8 May 1933, and Goebbels: *Tagebücher*, part I, vol. 2/III, p.182 (8 May 1933); 'at the request of Dr Oberfohren' and 'Dr Oberfohren's link', *Manchester Guardian*, 2 August 1933, cited in Bahar/Kugel: *Der Reichstagsbrand*, p.665f.; German edition in: BA Berlin R 3003/8, Bl. 82 (envelope).

48   'Already in one', memorandum, cited in: *Wer hat den Reichstag angezündet?*, p.4; 'He stated that' and 'a potential ban', minutes of ministers' meeting, 30 January 1933, 5.00 p.m.: BA Berlin R 43 I/1459, Bl. 244f.; 'in his despair', letter from Ida Oberfohren to Dr Ritthaler (no date), cited in Wolff: *Der Reichstagsbrand*, p.35.

49   For Heines, see Sack: *Der Reichstagsbrand*, p.48f.; 'Thus the cosy foursome', memorandum, cited in: *Wer hat den Reichstag angezündet?*, p.6; for the DNVP's supposed coup plan, see ibid., p.10, and Keil/Kellerhoff: *Gerüchte machen Geschichte*, pp.69–88.

CHAPTER 6

50   'As you know', 'As a result', 'organise and carry out' and 'The expenses', Münzenberg letter to the executive committee

of the Communist International, 12 June 1933, cited in *Reichstagsbrandprozess*, vol. 1, p.302f.

51 For the London counter-trial, see Pritt: *Der Reichtsagsbrand*, pp.13–42; for the panel's report, see ibid., pp.43–79; 'find the Nazis guilty', *Chicago Daily Tribune*, 16 September 1933; 'The Nazis are preparing', *New York Times*, 17 September 1933; 'Van der Lubbe is not a member', 'the documents' and 'The Reichstag was', Pritt: *Der Reichstagsbrand*, p.78f.

52 'The magnitude of', opening speech by Bünger, cited in *Reichstagsbrandprozess*, vol. 2, p.26; 'The focus in', *Berliner Morgenpost*, 22 September 1933; removal of van der Lubbe's chains: BA Berlin R 3003/16, Bl. 107a; see the indictment: BA Berlin R 3003/10; for van der Lubbe's life, see ibid. Bl. 9–13r; conspiracy in Neukölln, ibid. Bl. 21–8; spread of the fire, ibid., Bl. 32r–41; findings of the crime scene investigation, ibid., Bl. 52–61; 'The KPD's treasonous efforts', ibid. Bl. 106–10; 'What a morass', Thomas Mann to Wilhelm Kiefer, 26 October 1933, cited in *Frankfurter Allgemeine*, 30 October 2007.

53 'I do not want', handwritten note on the offer of a Dutch lawyer: BA Berlin R 3003/16, Bl. 79; for moving the court's venue to Berlin, see Cullen: *Der Reichstag*, p.244; battle of words Dimitroff–Göring, cited in *Reichstagsbrandprozess*, vol. 2, p.407f.

54 For Torgler's defending lawyer, see Sack: *Der Reichstagsbrand*, passim; 'As the available documents', report by Ritter: BA Berlin R 3003/56, Bl. 17–23; report by Wagner and Josse: BA Berlin R 43 II/294, Bl. 107–63, 199–293; report by Schatz: BA Berlin R 3003/56, Bl. 27–45; report by Brüning: BA Berlin R 3003/54, Bl. 4–10r, and addendum, ibid., Bl. 11r.

55 'The defendants', verdict cited in *Reichstagsbrandprozess*, vol. 2, p.878; 'Verdict in Leipzig', Goebbels: *Tagebücher*, part I,

vol. 2 III, p.343 (23 December 1933); 'miscarriage of justice' and 'final impulse', *Völkischer Beobachter*, 24 December 1933; 'protective custody', ibid. and *BZ am Mittag* (special edition), 23 December 1933.

56 For the intervention of the Dutch ambassador and for van der Lubbe's execution, see notes Wienstein: BA Berlin R 43 II/294, Bl. 439f.; for Torgler, see Schumacher: *M. d. R.*, pp.522–5; for Dimitroff, Popoff and Taneff, see Dimitroff: *Tagebücher*, vol. 2, pp.373–9, 593, 648.

CHAPTER 7

57 For the repairs in the Reichstag building, see Hahn: *Die Reichstagsbibliothek*, pp.365–402; 'We made it' and 'Disgraceful death', Foster et al.: *Reichstags-Graffiti*, p.80, 67; 'This is where', cited in Kellerhoff: *Ortstermin Mitte*, p.80f.

58 'It would have made', Nuremberg Trial, vol. 9, p.483; 'To put it briefly', 'A certain', 'As to how', 'What happened' and 'As far as', ibid., vol. 12, pp.276–8.

59 For Gisevius' detailed report, see Gisevius: *Bis zum bitteren Ende*, vol. 1, pp.13–126; for Gisevius' biography, see Weiß (ed.): *Biografisches Lexikon*, p.146; for a more detailed, yet more polemical account, see Tobias: *Reichstagsbrand*, pp.530–50; 'DNVP Leaders', *Völkischer Beobachter*, 10 June 1933; 'scheming careerist', Diels: *Lucifer ante portas*, p.198; 'covert communist', cited in Höhne: *Der Orden*, p.86; Gisevius on 20 July, see: Gisevius: *Bis zum bitteren Ende*, vol. 2, pp.358–416; for Gisevius' report on Stauffenberg's 'eastern sympathies', see Hoffmann: *Stauffenberg*, pp.472–4; 'pretends to' and 'All these claims',

Zeit, 11 November 1948, cited in Tobias: *Reichstagsbrand*, pp.548–50.

60 'I was', Diels: *Lucifer ante portas*, p.199f.; 'It has been proven', Wolff: *Der Reichstagsbrand*, p.41; 'astonishing lack of sources', 'On 28 February' and 'against their better judgement', ibid., p.25f.; for the criticism of Wolff, see Tobias: *Der Reichstagsbrand*, p.93f.; 'Even if a', Diels, cited in Tobias: *Der Reichstagsbrand*, p.5.

61 'Status, job and home', Tobias: *Der Reichstagsbrand*, p.3; Tobias the social democrat, see *Welt*, 8 February 2000; 'Of course I am', letter from Paul Franken to Fritz Tobias, 23 March 1965 (collection Kellerhoff).

62. 'Stand up, van der Lubbe!', *Spiegel*, 23 October 1959–6 January 1960; for Paul Karl Schmidt, see Benz: *Paul Carrell*, passim; 'He really took', *Spiegel*, 9 April 2001; for the Allensbach survey and the reaction in the press, see *Spiegel*, 23 December 1959; for the series overall, see Merseburger: *Augstein*, p.126f., 153, pp.390–6.

63. 'The Reichstag Fire: A Distorted Picture', *Zeit*, 4, 11, 18 and 25 March 1960; for the lawsuit Gewehr vs. Gisevius, see *Spiegel*, 25 January 1961, 24 January and 28 February 1962; 'financially ruined', Bahar/Kugel: *Der Reichstagsbrand*, p.792.

64. 'Allegedly personal' and 'ranging from', Tobias: *Der Reichstagsbrand*, p.530; for the lawsuit Gisevius vs. Tobias, see *Spiegel*, 24 January 1962; 'In humankind's', Tobias: *Der Reichstagsbrand*, p.592.

65. 'Cleverly and immediately' and 'less about the revision', Broszat: *Zum Streit*, p.276f.; 'unsuitable for publication', cited in Möller/ Wengst: *Zur Kontroverse*, p.555; 'The study that', Mommsen: *Der Reichstagsbrand*, p.411; 'This academic essay', *Spiegel*, 11 November 1965.

CHAPTER 8

66. 'The Reichstag Fire', 'Recently discovered' and 'had been able',
Telegraf, 23 December 1966; 'The Reichstag is', Calic (ed.): *Ohne
Maske*, p.69; for Hitler's attitude towards parliamentarianism,
see Hitler: *Mein Kampf*, pp.81–85, 296f., 659f.; for the plans
for 'Germania', see *Berliner Lokal-Anzeiger*, 12 April 1938, as
well as Kellerhoff: *Hitlers Berlin*, pp.124–31, and Reichhardt/
Schäche: *Von Berlin*, p.41f., 97, pp.99–101, 110–12, 127; for
Speer's report on Hitler's view on the Wallot building, see Speer:
Erinnerungen, p.166f.

67. 'First-class', *Zeit*, 21 February 1969; 'The transcriptions',
supposed report by Ludwig Krieger, cited in Calic (ed.): *Ohne
Maske*, p.15; according to Karl-Heinz Janßen, this sentence was
not in the original report, see Backes et al.: *Reichstagsbrand*, p.227;
'The first conversation', undated note, Alfred Deting, cited in
ibid., p.221; Trevor-Roper, see ibid., p.229; translation examples
cited in ibid., pp.223–5; 'Edouard Calic's book', cited in ibid.,
p.228; 'documents from', Schmädecke/Bahar/Kugel: *Der
Reichstagsbrand*, p.606, note 7.

68 'The depiction of', verdict, Supreme Court in Berlin,
7 February 1984 (collection Kellerhoff); for Calic's entry in
the Berlin telephone directory, see addendum to 1941 edition
of the telephone directory for the Reichspostdirektion district
in Berlin. Edition of March 1943, p.19: 'Calic, Edouard.
Auslandspressevertreter [foreign correspondent]. W 15,
Sächsische Str. 5. 920262', see also *Tagesspiegel*, 31 October 1979,
Zeit, 9 November 1979, and *Tagesspiegel*, 30 November 1979; for
Calic's biography, see Janßen: *Geschichte aus der Dunkelkammer*,
pp.31–40; for Calic's report about Wagner and the

Sachsenhausen concentration camp, see *Spiegel*, 17 November 1969, p.5.

69 'Potentially too biased', letter from Hans Mommsen to Sven Felix Kellerhoff, 18 November 2007 (collection Kellerhoff); 'International Committee', programme of the first symposium, cited in Backes et al.: *Reichstagsbrand*, pp.303–11; 'blackmail', 'disciplinary action' and 'I recommend', cited in ibid., p.109f.; for the committee's activities, see ibid., pp.88–114; 'ready to go', cited in Calic: *Der Reichstagsbrand*, p.441.

70 For the wrong accusation of Günther Zacharias, see Hofer et al.: *Der Reichstagsbrand*, vol. 1, p.278, *Spiegel*, 17 July 1972, as well as *Welt*, 18 and 19 July 1972; texts in the appendix: Hofer et al. (eds): *Der Reichtagsbrand*, vol. 2, pp.332–471; 'Prof Edouard Calic', Hofer/Graf: *Neue Quellen*, p.82.

71 'K-documents' in: Hofer et al. (eds): *Der Reichstagsbrand*, vol. 2, pp.366–87; 'The lads', ibid., p.366f.; for the refutation of the 'K-documents', see Backes et al.: *Reichstagsbrand*, pp.187–92; 'shortly after', 'details about' and 'I only learned', Rauschning: *Gespräche mit Hitler*, p.76f.; 'I know', Göring in: Nuremberg Trial, vol. 9, p.484.

72 'Löbe statement' in: Hofer et al. (eds): *Der Reichstagsbrand*, vol. 2, pp.442–8; 'I was in Breslau', ibid., p.444f.; 'Even later on', *Spiegel*, 9 December 1959; for the refutation of the 'Löbe statement', see Backes et al.: *Reichstagsbrand*, p.205f., as well as Hahn: *Die Reichstagsbibliothek zu Berlin*, p.289f.; for the library, see Löbe: *Erinnerungen*, p.149.

73 For the media debate between the *Zeit* and the *Tagesspiegel*, see *Zeit*, 9 and 23 November 1979, as well as *Tagesspiegel*, 31 October and 30 November 1979; see *Rheinischer Merkur*, 16 November 1979; 'As the committee' and 'so-called "original

documents"', Mommsen: *Rezension*, p.492f.; 'unprecedented insult', Hofer: *Erwiderung*, p.252f.

74 'The only purpose' and 'The signatories', press statement, 26 February 1986 (Walther Hofer and Christoph Graf), cited in Backes et al.: *Reichstagsbrand*, p.327; 'assumed that', letter from Christoph Graf to the *Bundesarchiv* [federal archive], Koblenz, 8 July 1986, cited in *Frankfurter Allgemeine Zeitung*, 9 January 1988 (reader letter by Hans Booms).

75 For the report by the criminal police in Zurich, see *Welt*, 18 September 1987; report printed in Hofer et al.: *Der Reichstagsbrand*, new edition, pp.472–84; critical comment in Henke: *Archivfachliche Bemerkungen*, pp.220–6; for the document of 1935, see *Frankfurter Allgemeine Zeitung*, 6 January and 9 January 1988; 'Orders received', Hofer et al.: *Der Reichstagsbrand*, new edition, inside front cover.

CHAPTER 9

76 'The documents', cited in copy of the handover confirmation in finding aid R 3003 ORA: BA Berlin, reading room, p.1; 'Mistakes occur', Fischler: *Fehlerliste*, p.2; see Schneider: *Neues vom Reichstagbrand*, p.38, footnote 5; 'Fischler wastes', Cullen: *Fischlers 'Forschungsergebnisse'*, p.3f.

77 *Rheinischer Merkur*, 10 December 1993; 'van der Lubbe had merely', Schmädeke: *Der Deutsche Reichstag*, p.106; for the in reality minor differences between the interrogations quoted by Schmädeke, see the original minutes: BA Berlin R 3003/1, Bl. 59f. as well as BA Berlin R 3003/6, Bl. 56.

78 'Hypnotised', Kugel: *Hanussen*, p.232, and Bahar/Kugel: *Der Reichstagsbrand*, pp.502–5; for Kugel, see *Welt*, 24 October 1998;

'newly discovered', *Neue Zürcher Zeitung*, 19 August 1995, as well as Bahar/Kugel: *Neue Aktenfunde*, p.823; 'Historians at Loggerheads again', *taz*, 21 February 1998; 'members of' and 'connection to', *taz*, 28 February 1998; see *Spiegel* special edition for the sixtieth anniversary, 8 January 2007; for Zacharias, see *Spiegel*, 17 July 1970 and 9 April 2001.

79 'This may not', 'personally encouraging' and 'protect the perpetrators', *Netzeitung*, 3 November 2000: http://www. netzeitung.de/deutschland/119643.html (last viewed 17 October 2007); 'list of sins' and '*Spiegel* version', *Neue Zürcher Zeitung*, 8 December 2000; 'a first-rate scandal', *Neues Deutschland*, 29 December 2000; 'belly flop' and 'scandal for', *Der Journalist* February 2001; for Augstein's award, see *Welt*, 14 May 2001, and *Spiegel*, 21 May 2001; 'It is right', *Berliner Morgenpost*, 14 May 2001.

80 'Further research', Schmädeke et al.: *Der Reichstagsbrand in neuem Licht*, p.651; *Welt*, 13 January–6 March 2000; article by Bahar/Kugel and Fischler in: *Berliner Morgenpost*, 13 and 27 February 2000; 'The act must have', Bahar/Kugel: *Der Reichstagsbrand*, inside front cover; *Neue Zürcher Zeitung*, 11 May 2001 and *Neues Deutschland*, 19 May 2001; 'The book does not', Mommsen: *Nichts Neues*, p.352; 'In a strange way', Hahn: *Replik*, p.2f.

81 'Unfortunately', *Frankfurter Allgemeine Zeitung*, 26 February 2003; see *Welt* and *Tagesspiegel*, 26 February 2003.

82 For the media debate between Bayrischer Rundfunk and *Spiegel*, see material in the Wiegrefe collection; 'So the *Spiegel* commissions', Brack/Hübner: *Der Reichstagsbrand*, p.7; interim injunction: order of regional court Hamburg, 20 March 2006, and verdict of regional court Hamburg, 2 June 2006; 'The statement', verdict of higher regional court, 6 March 2007;

'The German press council', letter from German press council to Hersch Fischler, 5 July 2007 (all Wiegrefe collection).

83 'Without being complete', Schneider: *Neues vom Reichstagsbrand?*, p.191; for the controversy between Fischler, Brack and Mommsen, see *taz*, 5, 19 and 26 November 2000, as well as *Netzeitung*, 12 February 2000: www.netzeitung. de/spezial/zeitgeschichte/124626.html (last viewed 17 October 2007).

84 In an action of 14 April 2011, Hersch Fischler denies having published Schneider's book. However, in the book it says, word-for-word: 'The editors (Hersch Fischler, Frauke Haag and Hans-Jörg Schneider) have reassigned or added to the superscripted numbering of annotations in a few instances.' ['Die Herausgeber (Hersch Fischler, Frauke Haag und Hans-Jörg Schneider) haben einige wenige Hochzahlen von Anmerkungsnummern genauer zugeordnet oder ergänzt.'] Schneider, *Neues vom Reichstagsbrand?*, p.54, annotation *. The action was dismissed.

85 'Helmut Krausnick felt', essay by Fischler in Schneider: *Neues vom Reichstagsbrand?*, p.51f.; 'ready for print', Calic: *Der Reichstagsbrand*, p.441; in the meantime, the text by Schneider has been published in Schneider: *Neues vom Reichstagsbrand*, pp.53–179; 'These statements', Möller/Wengst: *Zur Kontroverse*, p.555; 'interested in', letter Otto Dann, 24 May 2005 (collection Kellerhoff); 'new hypothesis', *Abenteuer Wissen*, ZDF, 11 July 2007.

CHAPTER 10

86 'The question', final report Zirpins: BA Berlin R 3003/1, Bl. 73; 'What is', Haungs: *Was ist mit den deutschen Historikern los?*, p.535; for Augstein, see Merseburger: *Augstein*, pp.7–11 and passim; for the *Institut für Zeitgeschichte*, see Möller: *Das Institut*, pp.1–69.

87 For van der Lubbe's hunger strike, see permission to force-feed: BA Berlin R 3003/2, Bl. 84f.; 'definite evidence', ongoing report by Commissar Bunge: BA Berlin R 3003/53, Bl. 3r; 'seized pieces', list: BA Berlin R 3003/109, Bl. 242–6.

88 For the attack on the radio station Gleiwitz, see Nuremberg Trial, vol. 2, p.497 and ibid., vol. 4, p.270f., as well as Domarus: *Hitler*, vol. 3, p.1,304f.; 'He thinks', Goebbels: *Tagebücher*, part I, vol. 9, p.237 (9 April 1941); 'I am convinced', Hitler: *Monologe*, p.161.

89 For the backdraft phenomenon, see Otto Widetschek: Backdraft (www.brandschutzforum.at/BFA/seiten/k-schutz/flash_rauchexplosion.htm; last viewed 21 October 2007) and Paul Grimwood: Flashover, Backdraft & Fire Gas Ignitions (http://www.firetactics.com/FLASHOVER%20&%20N.TECHS%20-%20METRIC.htm; last viewed 21 October 2007). 'Flashover' is seen as a different phenomenon among fire experts, namely the sudden ignition of all flammable surfaces in a room as a result of high radiant heat. However, 'backdraft' and 'flashover' are often inadvertently used interchangeably, as is the case in in Keil/Kellerhoff: *Deutsche Legenden*, p.64.

SOURCES AND BIBLIOGRAPHY

All archival materials used for the book are referenced in full in the notes; newspaper and magazine articles with the date of their respective editions; books with clear, short titles.

Archival Materials

Bundesarchiv Berlin [Federal Archive Berlin]
Collection R 43 Reichskanzlei
    I: 1459; 1460; 1465.
    II: 151; 294; 295; 398; 474; 1193; 1263; 1539.
Collection R 3003 Oberreichsanwalt beim Reichsgericht /
Reichstagbrand
    1; 2; 3; 4; 5; 6; 7; 8; 9; 10; 11; 16; 22; 34; 46; 52; 53; 54; 55; 56; 63;
    109; 225; 226; 227; 233.
Collection Dr. Klaus Wiegrefe, Hamburg

Material about the trial *Der Spiegel/Bayerischer Rundfunk* 2006/2007.
Collection Sven Felix Kellerhoff, Berlin
Collection of press cuttings (1933–2007); contemporary photos;
    correspondence, 1994–2007; varia, 1933–2007.

Newspapers and Magazines

Der Angriff; *Berliner Illustrierte*; *Berliner Lokal-Anzeiger*; *Berliner Morgenpost*; *Berliner Tageblatt*; *Berliner Zeitung*; *B.Z. am Mittag*; *Chicago Daily Tribune*; *Focus*; *Frankfurter Rundschau*; *Frankfurter Allgemeine Zeitung*; *Illustrierter Beobachter*; *Journalist*; *Junge Welt*; *Los Angeles Times*; *Neue Zürcher Zeitung*; *Neues Deutschland*; *New York Times*; *Reichsgesetzblatt*; *Der Spiegel*; *Süddeutsche Zeitung*; *Der Tagesspiegel*; *Die Tageszeitung*; *Telegraf*; *Völkischer Beobachter*; *Vorwärts*; *Vossische Zeitung*; *Die Welt*, *Weltwoche*; *Weserkurier*; *Die Zeit*.

Printed Sources

Abusch, Alexander: 'Das Braunbuch über den Reichstagsbrand',
    Weltbühne 2 (1947), pp.177–81.

Becker, Josef/Becker, Ruth (eds): *Hitlers Machtergreifung. Dokumente
    vom Machtantritt Hitlers 30. Januar 1933 bis zur Besiegelung des
    Einparteienstaates 14. Juli 1933*, 2nd ed. (München: 1993 [1983]).

Bonhoeffer, Karl/Zütt, Jürg: 'Über den Geisteszustand des
    Reichstagsbrandstifters Marinus von der Lubbe', *Monatsschrift
    für Psychatrie und Neurologie* 69 (1934), pp.675–93.

Booms, Hans/Repgen, Konrad (eds): *Akten der Reichskanzlei.
    Regierung Hitler* 1933–1938. Part I: 1933/34. Two vols
    (Boppard: 1983).

Braunbuch über Reichstagsbrand und Hitlerterror (Basel: 1933).

Braunbuch II. Dimitroff contra Göring. Enthüllungen über die wahren Brandstifter, 2nd ed. (Köln: 1981 [1934]).

Calic, Edouard (ed.): *Ohne Maske. Geheimgespräche Hitler-Breiting 1931* (Frankfurt/Main: 1968).

Delmer, Sefton: *Die Deutschen und ich* (Hamburg: 1962).

Diels, Rudolf: *Lucifer ante portas. Es spricht der erste Chef der Gestapo* (Stuttgart: 1951).

Dimitroff, Georgi: *Reichstagsbrandprozeß* (Berlin [East]: 1946).

—: *Tagebücher 1933–1943*. Edited by Bernhard H. Bayerlein. Two vols (Berlin: 2000).

Domarus, Max (ed.): *Hitler. Reden und Proklamationen 1932–1945*. Four vols, 4th ed. (Leonberg: 1988 [1962]).

Ebermayer, Erich: *Denn heute gehört uns Deutschland … Persönliches und politisches Tagebuch von der Machtergreifung bis zum 31. Dezember 1935* (Hamburg–Wien: 1959).

Engelbrechten, Julek [Julius] Karl von/Volz, Hans: *Wir wandern durch das nationalsozialistische Berlin. Ein Führer durch die Gedenkstätten des Kampfes um die Reichshauptstadt* (München: 1937).

François-Poncet, André: *Als Botschafter in Berlin*. German translation by Erna Stübel (Mainz: 1949 [1948]).

Gempp, Walter (ed.): *Berliner Feuerwehr. Dienstanweisung Feuerlösch- und Unfalldienst* (Berlin: 1931).

Gisevius, Hans-Bernd: *Bis zum bitteren Ende*. Two vols (Zürich: 1946).

Goebbels, Joseph: *Vom Kaiserhof zur Reichskanzlei. Eine historische Darstellung in Tagebuchblättern* (München: 1934).

—: *Die Tagebücher von Joseph Goebbels*. Part I. Notes 1923–1941. Edited by Elke Fröhlich. Nine vols (München etc: 1998–2006).

Hanfstaengl, Ernst: *Zwischen Braunem und Weißem Haus. Erinnerungen eines politischen Außenseiters*. 2nd ed. (München: 1970 [1970]).

Hitler, Adolf: *Mein Kampf.* Two volumes in one. 479–483rd ed.
 (München: 1939 [1925/26, and 1930]).

—: *Monologe im Führerhauptquartier 1941–1944.* Recorded
 by Heinrich Heims. Edited by Werner Jochmann
 (Hamburg: 1980).

Hofer, Walther (ed.): *Der Nationalsozialismus 1933–1945.* Revised
 ed. (Frankfurt/Main: 1963).

—/Calic, Edouard/Stephan, Karl/Zipfel, Friedrich (eds):
 Der Reichstagsbrand. Eine wissenschaftliche Dokumentation. 2 vols
 (Berlin/München: 1972–1978).

—/Calic, Edouard/Stephan, Karl/Zipfel, Friedrich (eds):
 Der Reichstagsbrand. Eine wissenschaftliche Dokumentation. Revised
 edition by Alexander Bahar (Freiburg: 1992).

Institut für Zeitgeschichte (ed.): *Widerstand als 'Hochverrat' 1933–1945*
 (München: 1994–1998) (microfiche edition).

Kantorowicz, Alfred: 'Der Reichstagsbrand. Auftakt zur
 Weltbrandstiftung', *Aufbau* 2 (1947), pp.111–18.

Kessler, Harry Graf: *Tagebücher 1918–1937.* Edited by Wolfgang
 Pfeiffer-Belli (Frankfurt/Main: 1961).

Löbe, Paul: *Erinnerungen eines Reichstagspräsidenten* (Berlin: 1949).

—: *Der Weg war lang* (Berlin: 1954).

Picker, Henry: *Hitlers Tischgespräche im Führerhauptquartier.* New ed.
 (Berlin: 1989 [1951]).

Pritt, Denis Nowell: *Der Reichstagsbrand. Die Arbeit des Londoner
 Untersuchungsausschusses* (Berlin [East]: 1959).

*Der Prozeß gegen die Hauptkriegsverbrecher vor dem Internationalen
 Militärgerichtshof Nürnberg 14. November 1945 bis 1. Oktober
 1946.* Forty-two vols (Nürnberg: 1948).

Rauschning, Hermann: *Gespräche mit Hitler* (Zürich/
 New York: 1940).

Reed, Douglas: *The Burning of the Reichstag* (London: 1934).

Der Reichstagsbrandprozeß und Georgi Dimitroff. Documents
27 February to 23 December 1933. Two vols (Berlin [East]:
1982–1989).

Sack, Alfons: *Der Reichstagsbrand-Prozeß* (Berlin: 1934).

Soer, Josh van (ed.): *Marinus van der Lubbe und der Reichstagsbrand*
(Hamburg: 1983).

Speer, Albert: *Erinnerungen* (Berlin: 1969).

Stresemann, Wolfgang: *Wie konnte es geschehen? Hitlers Aufstieg in der
Erinnerung eines Zeitzeugen* (Berlin: 1987).

Secondary Literature

Backes, Uwe et al. (eds): *Reichstagsbrand. Aufklärung einer historischen
Legende*. 2nd ed. (München–Zürich: 1987 [1986]).

Bahar, Alexander/Kugel, Wilfried: 'Neue Aktenfunde entlarven die
NS-Täter', *Zeitschrift für Geschichtswissenschaft* 43 (1995),
pp.823–32.

—: *Der Reichstagsbrand. Wie Geschichte gemacht wird* (Berlin: 2001).

—: 'Mommsens Nonsens', Reichstagsbrandforum (www.zlb.de/
projekte/kulturbox-archiv/brand/mommsens-nonsens.html;
last viewed 25 June 2007).

Benz, Wigbert: *Paul Carrell. Ribbentrops Pressechef Paul Karl Schmidt
vor und nach 1945* (Berlin: 2005).

Benz, Wolfgang/Distel, Barbara (eds): *Der Ort des Terrors. Geschichte
der nationalsozialistischen Konzentrationslager.* Vol. 2: *Die frühen
Lager. Dachau. Emslandlager* (München: 2005).

Berndt, Alfred: 'Zur Entstehung des Reichstagsbrandes. Eine
Untersuchung über den Zeitablauf', *Vierteljahreshefte für
Zeitgeschichte* 25 (1975), pp.77–90.

Bracher, Karl-Dietrich/Sauer, Wolfgang/Schulz, Gerhard: *Die
nationalsozialistische Machtergreifung. Studien zur Errichtung des*

totalitären Herrschaftssystems in Deutschland 1933/34 (Köln/ Opladen: 1960).

Brack, Gerhard/Hübner, Tobias: 'Der Reichstagsbrand – ein Kriminalfall aus der Geschichte', radio typescript, Bayerischer Rundfunk (München: 2006).

Bräutigam, Helmut/Gliech, Oliver C.: 'Nationalsozialistische Zwangslager in Berlin I. Die "wilden" Konzentrationslager und Folterkeller 1933/34', in Ribbe, Wolfgang (ed): *Berlin-Forschungen II* (Berlin: 1987), pp.141–78.

Broszat, Martin: 'Zum Streit um den Reichstagsbrand. Eine grundsätzliche Erörterung', *Vierteljahreshefte für Zeitgeschichte* 8 (1960), pp.275–9.

—: 'Nationalsozialistische Konzentrationslager 1933–1945', in Buchheim, Hans et al: *Anatomie des SS-Staates*, two vols (Freiburg: 1965), vol. 2, pp.7–160.

Burkert, Hans-Norbert/Matußek, Klaus/Wippermann, Wolfgang: *'Machtergreifung' Berlin 1933* (Berlin: 1982).

Calic, Edouard: *Der Reichstagsbrand. Die Provokation des 20. Jahrhunderts. Forschungsergebnis* (Luxemburg: 1978).

Cullen, Michael S.: *Der Reichstag. Parlament. Denkmal. Symbol* (Berlin: 1995).

—: 'Hersch Fischlers "Forschungsergebnisse" zum Reichstagsbrand – eine Replik', Reichstagsbrandforum (www.zlb.de/projekte/ kulturbox-archiv/brand/cullen.html; last viewed 25 June 2007).

Deiseroth, Dieter (ed.): *Der Reichstagsbrand und der Prozess vor dem Reichsgericht* (Berlin: 2006).

Eschenburg, Theodor et al.: *Der Weg in die Diktatur. Deutschland 1918 bis 1933* (München–Zürich: 1962).

Fest, Joachim: *Hitler. Eine Biographie* (Berlin/Frankfurt/Main: 1973).

Fischler, Hersch: 'Fehlerliste zu: Hans Mommsen: Der Reichstagsbrand und seine politischen Folgen',

Reichstagsbrandforum (www.zlb.de/projekte/kulturbox-
archiv/brand/fischler-fehler00.htm; last viewed 25 July 2007).

—: 'Hans Schneiders unvollendetes Manuskript "Neues vom
Reichstagsbrand?"', Reichstagsbrandforum (www.zlb.de/
projekte/kulturbox-archiv/brand/fischler_bwv.html; last
viewed 25 July 2007).

—: 'Zum Zeitablauf der Reichstagsbrandstiftung', *Vierteljahreshefte
für Zeitgeschichte* 53 (2005), pp.617–32.

—/Brack, Gerhard: 'Zur Kontroverse über den Reichstagsbrand',
Vierteljahreshefte für Zeitgeschichte 50 (2002), pp.329–34.

Giebeler, Marcus: *Die Kontroverse um den Reichstagsbrand.
Quellenprobleme und historiographische Paradigmen* (München: 2010).

Graf, Christoph: *Politische Polizei zwischen Demokratie und
Diktatur: die Entwicklung der preußischen Politischen Polizei
vom Staatsschutzorgan der Weimarer Republik zum Geheimen
Staatspolizeiamt des Dritten Reiches* (Berlin: 1983).

Gross, Babette: *Willi Münzenberg. Eine politische Biografie*
(Stuttgart: 1967).

Hahn, Gerhard: *Die Reichstagsbibliothek zu Berlin – ein Spiegel
deutscher Geschichte* (Düsseldorf: 1997).

—: 'Alte Legenden vom Reichstagsbrand. Wieder scheitert ein Buch
mit dem Versuch, die Mittäterschaft der Nazis zu beweisen.
Bislang unbekannte Dokumente werden nicht vorgelegt',
Reichstagsbrandforum (http://www.zeitreisen.de/kulturbox-
archiv/brand/hahn.htm; last view 22.6.2016).

—: 'Die Vorwürfe können belegt werden', Reichstagsbrandforum
(http://www.zeitreisen.de/kulturbox-archiv/brand/hahn-
replik.htm; last view 22.6.2016).

Haungs, Peter: 'Was ist mit den deutschen Historikern los? Oder:
Ist Quellen-Fälschung ein Kavaliersdelikt?', *Geschichte und
Gesellschaft* 13 (1987), pp.535–41.

Hehl, Ulrich von: 'Die Kontroverse um den Reichstagsbrand', *Vierteljahreshefte für Zeitgeschichte* 36 (1988), pp.259–80.

Henke, Josef: 'Archivfachliche Bemerkungen zur Kontroverse um den Reichstagsbrand', *Geschichte und Gesellschaft* 16 (1990), pp.212–32.

Hett, Benjamin C.: *Burning the Reichstag. An Investigation into the Third Reich's Enduring Mystery* (New York: 2014).

Hofer, Walther: 'Erwiderung', *Historische Zeitschrift* 236 (1983), p.252f.

—/Graf, Christoph: 'Neue Quellen zum Reichstagsbrand', *Geschichte in Wissenschaft und Unterricht* 27 (1976), pp.65–88.

Janßen: Karl-Heinz: *Geschichte aus der Dunkelkammer. Kabalen um den Reichstagsbrand. Eine unvermeindliche Enthüllung* (Hamburg: 1979).

Jesse, Eckhard: 'Die Kontroverse zum Reichstagsbrand – ein nicht endender Wissenschaftsskandal', *Geschichte und Gesellschaft* 14 (1988), pp.513–33.

—: 'Der Reichstagsbrand – 55 Jahre danach', *Geschichte in Wissenschaft und Unterricht* 39 (1988), pp.195–219.

—: 'Der Reichstagsbrand und seine "Aufklärer". Ein Fälschungsskandal geht zu Ende', in Corino, Karl (ed.): *Gefälscht! Betrug in Politik, Literatur, Wissenschaft, Kunst und Musik*, new ed. (Frankfurt/Main: 1996 [1988]), pp.106–27.

Karasek, Horst: *Der Brandstifter. Lehr- und Wanderjahre des Maurergesellen Marinus van der Lubbe, der 1933 auszog, den Reichstag anzuzünden* (Berlin: 1980).

Keil, Lars-Broder/Kellerhoff, Sven Felix: *Deutsche Legenden. Vom 'Dolchstoß' und anderen Mythen der Geschichte* (Berlin: 2002).

Kellerhoff, Sven Felix: *Mythos Führerbunker. Hitlers letzter Unterschlupf* (Berlin: 2003).

—: *Attentäter. Mit einer Kugel die Welt verändern* (Köln–Weimar–Wien: 2003).

—: *Hitlers Berlin. Geschichte einer Hassliebe* (Berlin: 2005).

—: *Ortstermin Mitte. Auf Spurensuche in Berlins Innenstadt* (Berlin: 2007).

Kempner, Robert M.W.: 'Hermann Göring als Organisator des Reichstagsbrandes und das Wiederaufnahmeverfahren für Marinus von der Lubbe', in Wasserburg, Klaus/Haddenhorst, Wilhelm (eds): *Wahrheit und Gerechtigkeit im Strafverfahren. Festgabe für Karl Peters aus Anlass seines 80. Geburtstages,* (Heidelberg: 1984), pp.365–74.

Kershaw, Ian: *Hitler,* two vols (München: 1998–2000).

Kugel, Wilfried: *Hanussen. Die wahre Geschichte des Hermann Steinschneider* (Düsseldorf: 1998).

Leske, Horst: '"Notruf der Feuerwehr, guten Tag!". 150 Jahre Nachrichtenwesen bei der Berliner Feuerwehr', in *150 Jahre Berliner Feuerwehr 1851–2001* (Berlin: 2001), pp.66–75.

Longerich, Peter: *Die brauen Bataillone. Geschichte der SA* (München: 1989).

Lottmann, Eckart: *Berliner Feuerwehr. Auf der Drehleiter der Geschichte* (Berlin: 1996).

McMeekin, Sean: *The Red Millionaire. A Political Biography of Willi Münzenberg, Moscow's Secret Propaganda Tsar in the West* (New Haven–London: 2003).

Merseburger, Peter: *Rudolf Augstein. Biografie* (München: 2007).

Möller, Horst: 'Das Institut für Zeitgeschichte und die Entwicklung der Zeitgeschichtsschreibung in Deutschland', in Möller, Horst/ Wengst, Udo (eds): *50 Jahre Institut für Zeitgeschichte. Eine Bilanz* (München: 1999), pp.1–69.

—/Wengst, Udo: Zur Kontroverse über den Reichstagsbrand', *Vierteljahreshefte für Zeitgeschichte* 49 (2001), p.555.

Mommsen, Hans: 'Der Reichstagsbrand und seine politischen Folgen', *Vierteljahreshefte für Zeitgeschichte* 12 (1964), pp.351–413.

—: 'Rezension zu: Walter Hofer u. a.: Der Reichstagsbrand. Eine wissenschaftliche Dokumentation', *Historische Zeitschrift* 233 (1981), pp.490–4.

—: 'Nichts Neues in der Reichstagsbrandkontroverse. Anmerkungen zu einer Donquichotterie', *Zeitschrift für Geschichtswissenschaft* 49 (2001), pp.352–7.

Podewin, Norbert/Heuer, Lutz: *Ernst Torgler. Ein Leben im Schatten des Reichstagsbrandes* (Berlin: 2006).

Pyta, Wolfram: *Hindenburg. Herrschaft zwischen Hohenzollern und Hitler* (München: 2007).

Raithel, Thomas/Strenge, Irene: 'Die Reichstagsbrandverordnung. Grundlegung der Diktatur mit den Instrumenten des Weimarer Ausnahmezustandes', *Vierteljahreshefte für Zeitgeschichte* 48 (2000), pp.413–60.

Reuth, Ralf Georg: *Goebbels* (München: 1990).

Schierz, Hans-Jörg: 'Von der Rädertine zum City-LHF. Die Entwicklung des Löschfahrzeugs', in *150 Jahre Berliner Feuerwehr 1851–2001* (Berlin: 2001), pp.54–62.

Schmädecke, Jürgen: *Der Reichstag. Geschichte und Gegenwart eines Bauwerks*. New ed. (München–Zürich: 1994 [1970]).

—: 'Die Reichstagsbrand-Kontroverse geht weiter', Reichstagsbrandforum (www.zlb.de/projekte/kulturbox-archiv/brand/schmnaedecke1999.2.1.html; last viewed 19 August 2001).

— /Bahar, Alexander/Kugel, Winfried: 'Der Reichstagsbrand in neuem Licht', *Historische Zeitschrift* 269 (1999), pp.603–51.

Schneider, Hans et al.: *Neues vom Reichstagsbrand? Eine Dokumentation. Ein Versäumnis der deutschen Geschichtswissenschaft* (Berlin: 2004).

Schouten, Martin: *Marinus van der Lubbe. Eine Biographie* (Frankfurt/Main: 1999).

Schumacher, Martin: *M. d. R.: Die Reichstagsabgeordneten der Weimarer Republik in der Zeit des Nationalsozialismus*. 3rd ed. (Düsseldorf: 1994).

Stojanoff, Petr: *Der Reichstagsbrand. Die Prozesse in London und Leipzig* (Verlag: Wien, Frankfurt, Zürich: 1966).

Tobias, Fritz: *Der Reichstagsbrand. Legende und Wirklichkeit* (Rastatt: 1962).

Wilke, Jens-P.: 'Zwischen allen Fronten', in *150 Jahre Berliner Feuerwehr 1851–2001* (Berlin: 2001), pp.78–83.

Wippermann, Wolfgang: 'Oberbranddirektor Walter Gempp: Widerstandskämpfer oder Krimineller? Kein Beitrag zur Reichstagsbrandkontroverse', in Ribbe, Wolfgang (ed.): *Berlin Forschungen 3* (Berlin: 1988), pp.207–29.

Wolff, Richard: 'Der Reichstagsbrand 1933. Ein Forschungsbericht', *Aus Politik und Zeitgeschichte*, vol. 3/56, pp.25–52.

ACKNOWLEDGEMENTS

It is always worth going for a walk at Lake Starnberg. This book too owes its existence to many hours of passionate discussions at this beautiful spot in Bavaria. It was Prof. Hans Mommsen who prompted me to write an objective and factual account of the events surrounding the Reichstag fire for the arson attack's seventy-fifth anniversary. I would like to thank him for his encouragement, as well as his willingness to write the introduction.

The transfer of power to the Nazis on 30 January 1933 – generally misleadingly termed 'seizure of power' – and their subsequent conquest of power has been an interest of mine for twenty years. In connection with the subject of the Reichstag fire, I also became acquainted with Prof. Henning Köhler, who taught me a lot about the importance of source criticism.

After I published my first newspaper article about the Reichstag fire, I received a friendly letter from Fritz Tobias. Since then, we have frequently met in Hanover for discussions about the Reichstag fire and the Nazi regime. Our opinions differed on some issues, but on others, we came to the same conclusions. I admire his energy – he has researched the subject of the Reichstag fire for more than half a century, and during that time has had to defend himself against incredibly malicious attacks, yet he has never lost heart.

Over the years, I engaged with the Reichstag fire in various newspaper articles and essays, as well as the books *Hitlers Berlin* and *Attentäter*. However, what was still missing was a comprehensive account that was unencumbered by the premise of the Nazis as the supposed culprits, and that also included the files from the federal archive. I would like to thank the archivists at the federal archive for their helpful assistance, which made it possible for even a busy newspaper editor like myself to thoroughly study the files once more.

As with all of my books about themes connected to Berlin, the Berlin-Studien collection at the Zentral- und Landesbibliothek [central and state library] Berlin proved invaluable. The microfilms of the Berlin newspapers of the time were also incredibly useful.

I extend my thanks to my colleagues at *Der Spiegel* and *Spiegel-TV*, Dr Klaus Wiegrefe and Michael Kloft, who generously offered their support.

I would also like to thank Wieland Giebel for his encouragement and understanding at the right time. The support of Lars-Broder Keil, Dr Lothar Wackermann and Stefan Kirschner was once again invaluable. Thanks also to Ulrich Hopp, the publisher at be.bra publishing house, who was enthusiastic about the project from the start, and Dr Robert Zagolla, who dedicatedly supported it. I was impressed by Martin Regenbrecht's excellent copy-editing.

Last but not least I would like to thank my family: my mother Jutta Kellerhoff, my father Peter Kellerhoff, Anna-Maria Lorenz and my sister-in-law Dr Tina Kellerhoff. I dedicate this book to my nieces Nelly and Clara, even though they will not be able to read this for a little while yet.

Sven Felix Kellerhoff

ABOUT THE AUTHOR

Sven Felix Kellerhoff was born in Stuttgart in 1971, and grew up in West Berlin. He studied history and media law, primarily at the Freie Universität Berlin, and is a graduate of the Berliner Journalisten-Schule. He has worked as a journalist since 1993, focusing on contemporary history. He has worked for Axel Springer Verlag in various roles since 1997, including science editor and culture editor at the *Berliner Morgenpost*. He has been senior editor for contemporary and cultural history for the WELT group since 2003. He was awarded the Hohenschönhausen-Preis 2012 (jointly with Erich Loest). He has written more than twenty books about contemporary German history.

You may also be interested in …

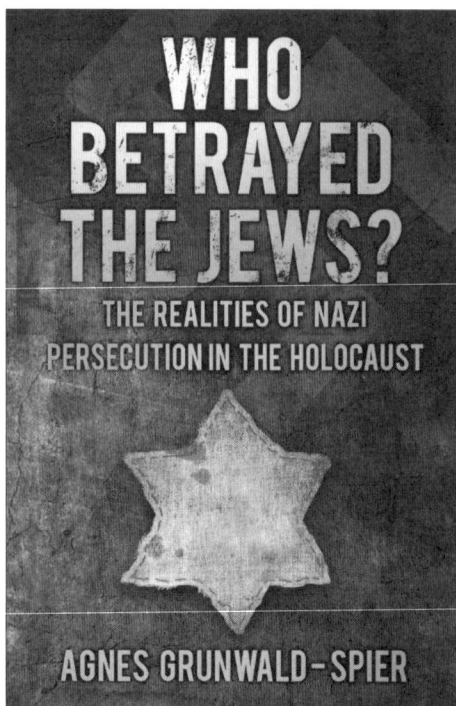

978 0 7509 5364 1

A groundbreaking study examing the various ways Jews were betrayed by their fellow countrymen during the Holocaust.

You may also be interested in …

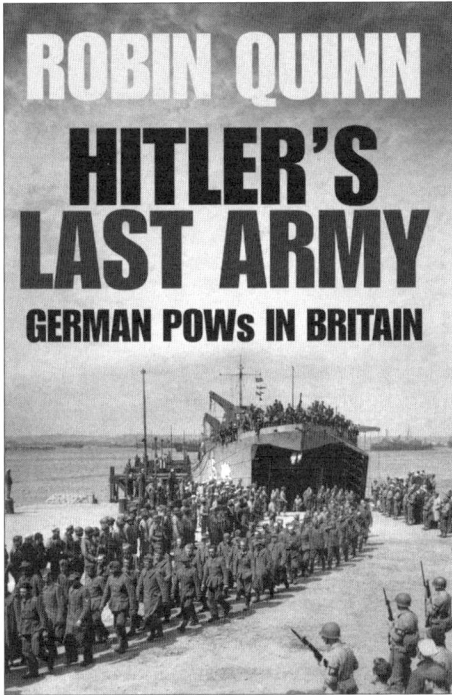

ROBIN QUINN

HITLER'S LAST ARMY

GERMAN POWs IN BRITAIN

978 0 7524 8275 0

A fresh perspective on the experiences of the Second World War including exclusive interviews with former German POWs, and extensive archive material.

The History Press

The destination for history
www.thehistorypress.co.uk

You may also be interested in …

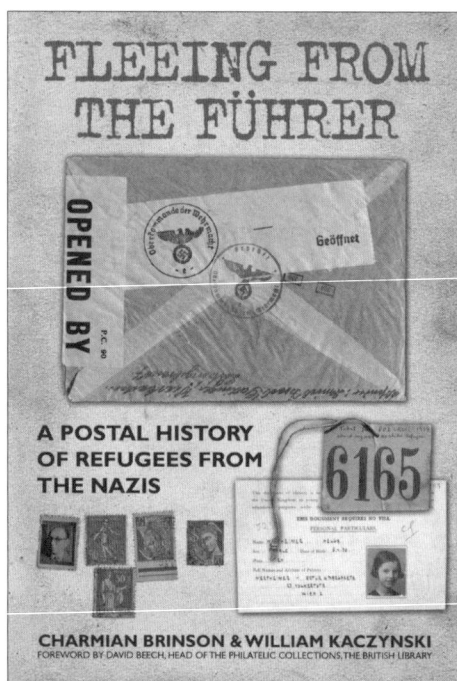

978 0 7509 6188 2

An unusual collection of correspond-
ence that shows the incredible nature
of this worldwide emigration and the
indomitable spirit of these refugees.